# Cosmin-Stefan Georgescu

## *Hamlet Badly Acted*

## *Aphorisms*

© 2022 **Europe Books**| London
www.europebooks.co.uk | info@europebooks.co.uk

ISBN 9791220120005
First edition: October 2022

**Hamlet Badlay Acted
Aphorisms**

While waiting for your happiness you are standing. That is why you have the feeling it is late.

Where are the happy people coming back? I would like to go in that direction.

I have thousands of 'likes' but nobody loves me.

'Yes' may be a refusal if you do not keep your promise.

You cannot live with happiness in the same house, let alone in the same bed.

Peace, even when it comes after another peace, brings about joy.

Venus of Milo has no arms. Her legs are long enough, though.

The way you kill time is in fact, the way you kill yourself.

Life takes by surprise only those people who live it.

Life never gives us what we want, but it takes what we could have wished for.

If you try to preserve happiness, you lose it.

Unhappiness fights against oblivion better than happiness does.

Most men got inebriated with scent not wine.

We are not born immortal, but we can become.

Many people are not impressed by happiness, when it is other people's happiness.

The real victory is in what all the others have failed.

If an enemy fear you - you are your own enemy.

Love is a sheet music played with four hands, which in time it played on two pianos.

The After Life is made up of our unlived moments in this World.

Who wants to be happy in this world needs a soft pillow.

School does not teach you what to do, it teaches you what other people have done.

Interest is the mask of love.

The Time of Death is limitless. That is why it takes charge of glory.

We are only a part of what we should be.

Happiness is evanescent in order to avoid becoming dull/uninteresting.

Whoever wishes us, "Bon appetite" is the person who has cooked the meal.

Quite often, two people who love each other have different reasons for doing it.

When love grows old it moves from heart to brain.

Waiting with no hope is a waste of time.

When it comes to happiness, we are some vessels riddled with bullets.

Resignation is a mild version of failure.

We read less than people write but this is a big advantage.

"Yes" is a kind of no if you do not keep your promise.

Like all the people who are concerned about themselves, I am wasting my time, but I think otherwise.

Life is a race to death while hoping we are running away from it.

You are old when the lived years do not allow you to be young any longer.

There is a big difference between love at first sight and love at first glance!

Every day prove to yourself that you are still capable of loving!

Hares-both among hares and wolves-sleep light.

A circle and a sphere always complete for perfection.

If a begger no longer begs for himself/herself, it means that he/she has privatized.

I am universal. I love any human.

If you dismantle me - I am different.

If only injuries learnt from smile how to disappear.

I weep like a weeping willow.

Nothing of what our soul loves leaves us untouched.

Any happiness transforms into its opposite!

Happiness is like submerging. You cannot resist long like this.

All love declarations past midnight are indecent.

If happiness were contagious, I would accept to be vaccinated.

If they had had cameras when Vinci lived, Gioconda' s husband would have taken a photo of her.

Love! Someone will love you back!

We are the earthworms of some amateur fishers.

For some time even happy experiences have been the same.

In a competition it is not important what your position is when you start, only your finishing position.

Few are the people who are happy because other people are happy.

If you are patient any of your wishes will come true but much later for you than for the others.

People are like wells. You have to fill with water many buckets and lift them up before you could come across fresh water.

A man who loves a woman loves all the others. A woman who loves a man detests all the others.

When you ask for a divorce, you do not have to come with your wife. When you marry you must.

You cannot get a divorce every time you do not like the food. For love you should not make concessions.

If it were only for the honeymoon, one should still get married

I am the sultan asking Sherezade to get it over with the stories.

When we are in love, we call each other's first names so loudly that the porch churches resound.

If God forgives us, it does not mean us repeating the mistake.

Love is death with offspring.

Live on earth as you might be living in Heaven and both Earth and Heaven will thank you.

We can speak about happiness only when we do not know what it really is.

Judging by how much I love I could have become a cardiologist.

Poetry does not belong the paper, but the beloved person's heart.

When one writes, they should write for the illiterate people, too.

No happiness can make you happy twice.

We are more romantic when dressed up for the ball, but we are thinking about the pyjamas.

When we love we start with those who are not worthy of it.

A bride cries when she leaves her house, but she does not take with her all her belongings.

They drink as much wine both at a wedding reception and a funeral.

In autumn no flower can resist the temptation of dying.

All my watches have stopped. I look great wearing only one, though.

Never give up any of your loves! You never know which one of them will last.

Contemporary period does not mean the same time but the same ideas.

No flower blooms for itself.

Love for your enemy is narcissical.

Happiness without love is like rum flavour without cake.

A billet-doux without lyrics is just a good-bye letter.

Something that does not make you hurry gives you patience.

A volcano does not get extinct with water.

The moment you imagine life is only yours is the beginning of its failure.

When in doubt whether you live or dream - check whether you are wearing your pyjamas.

The only serious thing you can do with your life is to live it.

I - that side of me that has the veto right.

I have loved my life more than it has loved me.

Autumn is the season when each and every leaf tries to become a tree of its own.

Life never gives us what we want, but it takes away what we could have wanted.

Only those who experience Hell on Earth will be admitted to Heaven in the Afterlife.

There are limited places on earth, that is why we have to mate.

Life relies on what we live.

All your dreams come true when you dream.

The most beautiful way of making love with a woman is to think about her.

A stag cannot run through a dense forest because of its antlers. It has to stay and fight.

I am the most unstable /the ficklest of the mortals. I die every day /I keep dying every day.

I miss only one person. It is the child I used to be.

Death always makes the final remark.

Love is a commandment two people have to observe.

Reconciliations are sadder than separations.

Life is what is left for you to do before you die.

I do not take on the consequences of what I write as everyone can understand it in his/her own way.

The soul is a vacant lot where lilies grow.

Who fights for justice fights for the people.

When two people quarrel you do not know who started.

The happier people are the more disunited they get.

Happiness does not absolve you of its consequences.

The gardener told me to mawn the lawn. I want your suggestion when you go to the Hairdresser's.

The most beautiful memories are those you keep secret.

Retro-fashion is being released.

I think I have noticed something about you. Put on your clothes, so I can show you.

You are fabulous. You are always the same age.

Dress in a summary way! I will take care of the contents.

I am an impostor. I love both you and me.

Each flower reminds me of you, particularly this unpicked one.

Try to forget me, you will see how difficult this is.

I am your lover whom you have not met yet.

Do you still have patience with me? I don't.

What are you doing tonight? With whom?

You look better in your slim fit jeans than in your wedding dress. Keep your jeans on!

I have pawned my soul. With the money I have bought flowers for you.

If you are a virgin, don't be afraid. All flowers are like that at the beginning of spring.

Give me love, not flowers! Flowers fade.

As soon as I am happy, I get hold of a memory.

Don't turn halfway for any petty reason! If the cat is not black it does not foretell anything bad.

We are growing up. We should metamorphose instead.

If I were a painter, I would create some new colours.

I love you all. If I did not I could not look you in the eyes.

He who sets you free only loose the loop.

Words soon become an echo. Silence always does it.

When God gives you a helping hand someone has been praying for you.

I see the world through a field glass. The field glass is mine. The world is not.

If you are a gunpowder barrel, plunge into water not fire.

I am empathetic with me.

While I am waiting, I become dreamy not angry.

Once our homework was to fall in love.

I was kicked out of school. They were whitewashing it.

When I fell in love, I did not do it to see how it was like, I did it because I was loving.

If I were a pirate, I would ask whether there are books on the ship.

The way you make love defines you better than the way you hate.

When you are sleeping with a beautiful woman it does not mean you are an insomniac.

Do not deal with anything transient apart from the fruits of the earth!

In the justice you hope there is always a reward you think you deserve.

A nude is love's finery.

It is boredom not hatred that opposes love.

The moral of the Genesis is the following: you cannot do everything in one day.

You should consider yours even the happiness you did nor enjoy.

When you forget you get younger than your memories.

Peace is always a reason to feel happy even when it comes after another peace.

Gioconda is smiling because she has understood life. If she had defeated it, she would have laughed.

I do not have the strength to be happy, but I do have the weakness to admit it.

You cannot stop the Sun when the shade is an advantage to you.

When you start playing a game of cards do not boast with your readings, first ask how many aces there are.

Love your enemy. Even if he kills you, he will weep your grave.

I am as weak as an ant but one day I will find the anthill.

We are more transient than the autumn leaves. That is why so many things can impress us.

Only one menagerie would not be enough to hold my wilderness.

Happiness is not what is happening to you, it is what is happening to the others while you believe it is happening to you.

I have nor had ambitions. Nevertheless, there have been people who called them so.

It is happiness itself that works against itself giving birth to melancholy.

On one dish of a balance lay your sorrows and satisfactions and on the other your soul. The scales will balance.

The light in your heart comes from your soul, too.

I am only that part of me that is invisible.

I was the first to abandon myself.

Only when you do not take the responsibility for a good deed it becomes a good deed.

I will not be happy. I will be as you people want me to be.

Do not count your wrinkles. It was not you who made them appear.

One cannot build a future out of memories.

We are weaker than our dreams although their texture is diaphanous.

Humans' patience is weaker than Gods and this leads to a conflict.

If you tiptoe you are not taller, you are more attentive.

I am a spider concerned with setting free what I catch in my web.

People who come back from a war are at war with those who did not participate.

Life is an island. By its end you have to learn how to swim.

There are many people here on Earth who pray to God hoping their prayer will be heard by those who could solve it.

I have made a pact with me to get on well with you.

In love one has to wait for nine months the longest.

When someone says they love you do not formalize.

You cannot get out of solitude by yourself.

The fiercer a feline is the fluffier/velvetier.

Life is a permanent disappointment to which you should not pay attention.

Waiting is the kindest death.

When you turn around, the road turns around with you.

The executioner arrives at the scaffold before the victim.

When you are in a hurry even eternity can make you angry.

There are so many saints around God-nevertheless, we all address Him.

We set our heart upon time hoping it is the same with eternity.

If happiness takes you by surprise, you do not deserve it I do not have wings but elytra.

Sorrow gives you the chance of being happy again.

Life is not what happens to others it is what happens to you.

Is that happiness real if it only belongs to you?

Health is when you tell a doctor to wear a scarf if he/she does not want to catch a cold.

A poem is a soul, a single soul, that is alone like a bird in a forest after migratory season.

When I was little, I used to do my homework. These days I have misplaced it.

People who read only good books complain that for a long time they haven't read anything.

Don't sacrifice anything to those who want you to be sacrificed.

People stopped going a-carolling and taking with them a whip.

I do hope that out of so many happy moments there is one only for me.

There is so much carelessness when we hope we will be able to forget.

When you defeat someone, you defeat them together with their mother, so you'd better ask them for forgiveness.

Not all people who tell the truth are right.

The Amazons are so exquisite that they don t have to have two breasts.

The more you love the more unfaithful you are to whom you loved first.

Your sufferings hurt me more than my own as I don't know how intense they are.

You'd better have no expectation. Enjoy the latest one!

Go on your path as long as no one else does it!

Only what you have experienced in your life gives it a meaning.

How many happy people does it take to make a country?

I left my country the same as I left my mother's womb.

You have a wonderful start in your life if your mother is a loving woman.

If you want God to hear your prayer and grant it, you must pray several times.

If you miss me, it is because I miss you.

When my sweethearts had a congress, I was elected vice-president.

If we want to be happy, we have to do our best in advance.

We owe life our life sentence.

Don't worry! Happiness doesn't last long either!

What happens to the mortals doesn't happen to gods.

No other deception is greater than thinking you have overcome it.

Whether you remember a happy or a sad moment you feel regret all the same.

Soul is crazier than mind.

When I was young, I thought I was mature. Now I think the other way round.

If I told you how much I love you, but I am afraid you might love me more.

You don't miss people you loved, you miss people you didn't love enough.

Antum glory is just appreciation.

Whenever I made a mistake, I was young.

God banished us from heaven not because of what we did, but because of what we could have done.

Ancient Greeks believed that it was only destiny that was against you.

Our mind is our soul exiled outside our heart.

If fate loved us, we would stop loving each other.

If you dig a pit for someone else, don't do it too deep! It is for you.

One can live well on holy water and communion bread in the After Life.

I began to feel happy when I realized I couldn't help it.

The difference between a mortal and an immortal is the way they worship a tomb.
The fruit of chance is always unripe.

The place of sacrifice is in the heart.

Every waiting is a procrastination.

I'm the manager of lost hopes. I won't accept them written on paper.

The more impressive your CV is, the sooner you'll disappoint the others.

I've tried so many things in my life that in the After Life I'll be bored stiff.

A mistress doesn't love you; she puts you to the test.

Flowers which bear fruit are the first to bloom.

For a dying man eternity is tomorrow.

The same sun which blinds us gives us the light.

Man has only a few feelings, but he makes such a fuss about them!

Waiting, not moment is time's measuring unit.

I was asked to attend the conferences bringing with me all the books I have written. They have changed their mind and asked me to bring my Muses.

God forgives all your trepasses, but you don't forgive your enemies' similar one

I'm the manager of lost hopes. I won't accept them written on paper.

A mistress doesn't love you, she puts you to the test.

I've got more patience than time.

If you get bored while waiting, you are not waiting for something or someone you really want.

I'm more falling than the star of o mortal man.

I sometimes feel like telling the truth for a change.

A writer starts speaking when he writes down.

He whose future is ensured doesn't live, he fills in a form.

I write a lot of balderdash to unburden myself.

I haven 't met immortal people who need a doctor.

I've always spoken too much. Now I write too much.

I'd like to isolate myself on an island, but all of them are already continents.

Writing is my worst addiction. I have some more equally inexcusable.

Don't waste your time reading me! You'd better buy my books.

What will you do when you are busy if you read in your spare time?

When you move a piece on a chess board, out of one thousand thoughts only one must be carried out.
We feel closer to history which is outside us than to chemistry which is inside us.

When you are praised, it is like you borrow money with the highest interest rate.

A divorce is in fact a separation before the others.

If your future were only yours, it would be unbearable.

When you believe in what you do is like you pray working.

The mirror of one's soul is another soul.

A word of love is not echoed.

Sadness seems greater in beautiful eyes.

When the thought is sad the word is in mourning.

If you are afraid of precipices, you are afraid of tall bridges, too.

No heart is roomy enough for a love.

Without blood we wouldn't know when we are wounded.

I live in the depth of an incomprehensible thought.
I am not what you can see.

I start a game of chess without the King.

You are forever in love with what you used to love.

You look great when you don't ask questions.

Women use lipstick between courses.

I have a problem: my girlfriends have very beautiful friends.

I'd give up writing if I knew what else I could take up.

Snails and I share the same unit of time.

When will our unlived experiences come to an end?

I fall in love easily. All I have to do is to look at myself in the mirror.

You can feed a giraffe from your hand only if it bows down its head.

I was expelled from school when I fell in love because they didn't know who I loved.

You are more likely to be in danger if you are prideless.

I was born in România but for a short time.

Curiosity has distorted the keyhole a lot.

I have been alone all my life, but I still haven't had enough of it.

They don't expel you from hell. You must run away from there.

If pride is on your side, it won't allow you to win.

There are a lot of lonely women in the street. All of them wear a wedding ring.

Nobody stands me with my ambitions. I can't stand myself without them.

My hope is that you all have, at least, one hope.

If you speak without being asked, no one listens to you.

Your friends are only the kids you played with, when you were little.

Happiness exemption is a right of mortals unanimously unclaimed.

If at least one of my hopes had come true, I would have given up on all the others.

Happiness is a way of wasting your time, but sadness doesn't give it back to you either.

If the lie told a single truth, it would compromise itself forever.

At a certain age it no longer matters how old you are. People give you what you ask them, God gives you what you deserve.

Good things are never enough, not even for those who deserve them.

I asked happiness to leave me alone and it allowed me to fall in love.

The soul surpasses the body. Any sail of a ship is worth one thousand rows.

I leave time alone, hoping it will do the same with me.

Buttetflies have to eat leaves, before they can land on flowers.

My sweetheart is not made out of one of my ribs but of my whole body.

I have given myself so many bad advice that I am glad I have followed none.

What happened to Adam and Eve happens to us again: we spend in heaven only the first part of our life.

There is a spring in the eyes, winter should take account of.

In vain can you fly if you cannot land.

Fashion shows you what is wearable not what clothes you should put on.
If you are impatient in the church, what will you do in the After Life?

I miss you in everything that happens to me.

It is so warm in my heart that you don't have to put on your clothes.

If either Adam or Eve had stayed in Heaven, they wouldn't have brought the Hell on earth.

I wish I were a bit older to see what it is like to be young.

If you want to love the same man/woman all your life, you must fall in love with him /her every day.

Don't admit you failed until your next victory.

If you marry only at registry office, you are half divorced.

No one understands the world. I admit it.

I write for all those who can read.

Don't get ready for a long conversation with someone who doesn't know how to listen.

Give up writing not because they don't read you, but because you have run out of ideas.

The only person I'm impatient with, it's me.
Communist queues taught me how to be patient in capitalism.

Life leaves you behind, and your deeds must catch up with it.

There are still several mistakes I didn't make in my youth.

You are young because it becomes you, not because you intend to.

It takes much time to be unhappy.

Never believe the one who says is busy! Believe the one who is working!

The sun is up. See? It's important to knock on the door at night.

We are so happy when we are as if we have never been before.

You cannot be happy on your own.

How quickly people forget what they ought to remember!

The greatest mistake when you are in love is to believe you are loved.

Silence is not about saying nothing, but about understanding everything.

Powder your life if you want it to fit in a sandglass.

I had access to happiness. It was not mine.

We make promises as if we intended to keep them.

Desire plays havoc among all the other feelings.

When I finally admitted God was right, it was too late. He had already proved it to me.

If I come back, it means I have never left.

In the beginning Heaven couldn't stand just two people, now it is ready to admit all of us.

The only being that detests himself/herself is the human.

I am patient but not a moment longer.

Only my memories succeeded in defeating me.

In time, to stay young is the only alternative.

I need me to be me or I need me to be complete.

What is strange is not that I have hopes but that they come true.

On the day you do nothing you fail to be happy.

If Zeus loves you, he puts pebbles in your sandglass.

Since Archangel Gabriel a good piece of news has been brought personally.

Love doesn't teach you anything good but helps you forget bad things.

Doctors lose patience with healthy patients.

Vanity is pride without ambition.

God has created the world for a reason, but He didn't tell us what it is.

Two days in a row without the night between them would be unbearable.

It is not enough to revolt, you must be right too.

You cannot lose something that didn't belong to you, but you can lose something you wish for.

Eternity is not a period of time, it is a memory.

It's not enough to forgive your enemy, you must help him/her forgive himself /herself.

If all actors took their roles seriously, after each performance of the play "Hamlet" they would need a new cast.

No day is only yours.

The time for love should not be wasted on anything else.
When I succeed someone is happy and sad at the same time. My mother.

What I loved was not enough. The piece of evidence: I still love.

You must pray only when you are on your own, otherwise God is not present.

Nobody is contemporary with his/her own life.

Any mortal would give his/her immortality in heaven for an extra day on earth.

Even the optimist people need to be encouraged.

You should start fasting when you are hungry not full.

If the lioness had a mane, it would be the queen of animals.

Sunday is the shortest day.

Let me sleep where your longing takes a rest!

If you have decided to postpone, it's better to wait.

Don't indulge yourself in being indifferent! Do something more!

God banished people from the Garden of Eden for them to make a new one somewhere else.

It is not illness that defeats us, but our fear.

Springs are so afraid of florist's shops.

I prefer words to moments of silence.

It is difficult to be alive and eternal at the same time.

The chance of my lifetime is my birth.

If I took my exams once again, I wouldn't get any prizes.

If you need more granite for the pedestal than for the statue, you are famous.

A divorce is successful if the two parties exchange their addresses.

When you receive a piece of news you don't know whether it is good or bad.

When I said, "Enough with happiness", I fell in love.

You age faster If you do nothing.

The voice of ignorance sounds louder than a clap of thunder.

If you have only one day to live, pray for one more.

If we want our soul to ascent to Heaven, we must love with it while on Earth.

You can be eternal, but it takes time.

As long as you are in Heaven, it no longer matters how you got there.

The snowdrops of my temples have bloomed. Spring plays havoc among my girlfriends.

It has taken me some time to live.

When your body cries do you still need your soul?

Love your enemies as long as you still have them!

The black widow has invited me to dinner.

No love is only yours.

I treasure the moment like a watch.

Hope doubles chances of implementation.

A soul is smaller than the love it contains.

Forgive before you forget!

Only what you hate is always yours.

People would rather believe historians than futurologists.

I've grown old. White beard takes longer to shave.

My only girlfriend knows I'm being unfaithful to her.

My guardian angel told me: "I'm taking a nap as long as you aren't showing off"

That's how I have been loving: by looking around.

If you are not in some memories, at least there is your memory.

We have almost succeeded in snowing. It's a shame we fail its colour.

Let it snow over you! Something white will still persist.

Coffee hasn't tasted bitter since I gave up drinking.

I am as old as my memories are.

I haven't been unfaithful to you. You expected too much from me.

I've won. My girlfriend's name is not Eureka, though.

If you tell the truth to those who don't understand it, you harm him, and you harm them.

First of all, man spoils the world and then asks God for help.

The blood dripping from the time wounded by you is in fact yours.

Time has its share of guilt when we are late, but we are the guiltiest.

Time prefers life to death since the latter competes with it.

Time is the stopwatch which stops when we stop running.

Time makes an appointment with us whenever it suits it, as it is used to waiting

I'm afraid that my sweetheart comes to the Full Moon nights.

The only thing that remains after happiness is its bitter aftertaste.

We have been given sleep to behave ourselves at night.

I dialled the number of that pink phone you used to answer, when you were taking a bath.

I know the shapes, but not the size.

Since no one would accept us embraced, we are walking hand in hand.

My hatred for you is our love's mystery.

I'd stay awake a whole night in your soul.

All the flowers I've unoffered my girlfriend, have taken roots inside her.

I buy a flower for my girlfriend every day. When she comes I'll offer her a herbarium.

One's soul can be dressed only by a good designer.

The coldness you love me with, honours me.

Beauty and Grace are one step apart.

Procrastination delays good things.

The only thing I have borrowed from Beauty is the right to not comprehend.

Beauty is never found where you have left it.

I owe it only to Love.

My glory is to take my time.

We'll be winners when we have no more enemies.

Don't stop where Destiny has abandoned you!

Judge what happens to you, but don't implement the sentences!

Allow me between you and me! There is enough room.

Announce your birth! Let it be done through someone else's voice though.

God would rather you obeyed Him, than prayed Him for something.

Not only is life short, but it also skips certain stages.

When Heaven gates open, they creak and it terrifies the devils.

When a hungry man asks for food, he speaks softly.

If your prayer is listened and granted, it was not God but the evil one who heard you.

Too much patience makes you forget what you are waiting for.

If Venus had had hands, the Louvre guard would have been reinforced.

What you still have after you share is sweeter.

Truth that disturbs is necessary.

I have all the defects associated with my age but no wisdom.

A single unrequited love is enough to compromise all the others.

It is worth taking picture of everything the heart cannot develop.

The number of happy moments cannot be counted, but they can make a whole day.

A school goes on living if its disciples, become mentors of other disciples.

The more sections the Hell has, the more it seems to be Heaven -like.

Happiness cannot be compared.

We live in a horizontalized sandglass.

The eyes cry. The cheeks get the worst of it.

We share the guilt of falling in love.

I'm the fall of snow turned into tears, by the Time it has touched the ground.

I got drunk with dozens of unopened bottles of wine in the galley in order to save the raft, useful in case of a shipwreck.

Allow being snowed, an extra angel keeps the drought away.

Love is the heart still beating long after we have left this world.

Only what doesn't happen will be considered novelty.

I am a Sun that no sunset leaves indifferent.

If they give you as an example, it no longer matter whether it is good or bad.

Your glory lasts as long as the others claim it.

Alas those who don't need Angels and have found devils who listen to them.

In everyday life happiness stays in your way.

No priority should be only yours!
Forgive the offender, stop the one who is about to trespass.

Mother-the icon in her children's eyes.

Spring starts when flowers pluck up courage.

If you want to be eternal, don't forget eternity started several millennia before you.

People didn't know what to do with Happiness, so they exchanged it for Love.

You need one single day to remember all the others.

You must like the deli before you taste it.

None of my girlfriend has proposed to me to be her boyfriend.

Of all my girlfriends, none of them has proposed to me to be her boyfriend.

I still have a long way to go before I become a sacred monster. I am just a monster.

It is not commendations I'm short of, but of sincere praises.

If you've got used to death, it means you have many more years to live.

No traitor works on his/her own.

Style is a moving grace.

If you want to teach someone, you must love him/her first.

Peace lasts until weapons are perfected.

I bet on future. The past catches up with you, no matter what.

One friend may leave you in need, but it is not right if all of them leave you.

Chance, in its turn, has its destiny.

People take the right to property for the right to happiness.

We've run out of questions; we keep rephrasing the same ones. The answers are different though.

Justice which hurts is unjust.

Only mean people impress when they are being good.

If you don't know what to do with your freedom, you are not free.

If you want to get younger, at a certain age you have to subtract the years you should add.

No matter what you feel, never lose your smile.

There are several ways of idling/ wasting your time. The most effective one is to start working.

Happiness takes advantage of us not to get bored.

I've left my youth to those who still want to love me.

Don't wait at a door beyond which they are having a meeting!

Time present is time past for some, and time future for some others.

You need patience when you wait for something good to happen.

It is more important who loves you, than for how long.

You get as much happiness as you give.

First you are glad, and then you are happy.

Let only those you can defeat, stand in your way!

Past is not only what you remember, future is not only what you imagine.

If the Sun woke up before you, it didn't do it on purpose.

Everything you expect to happen in the future was given to you in the past, but you didn't notice.

Don't tell the truth to those who know it, it will bore them. Don't tell it to those who don't know it, it will make them angry!

Forgive me, but don't put a blame on me!

When I have run out of truth, what else am I going to tell you?

One friend may leave you in need, but it is not right if all of them leave you.

Exception is an excuse for rule.

Love cannot afford an interest, so it borrows nothing.

An unbroken horse and a sincere feeling are more capricious when one reins them in.

Where Happiness tries, Unhappiness succeeds.

A day is made by a waking man not by the rising sun.

Hatred looks for reasons, love for feelings.

When the Sun sets it has got red for how much it has seen.

The wedding ring makes love circular.

The best parents-in-law are those who intend to ask for a divorce, but they don't.

Good manners have a low opinion of real pleasures.

There is only one Miron, but the sky is not enough for him.

You are always right when you tell the truth.

Every time we make a mistake, we don't regret the mistake, but the fact we have made it.

Everything that happens to you is only what you cannot postpone.

When people are alone, they learn how to love.

Consolation prizes have added platforms to a podium Disappointment is proportional to hope.

Misunderstood life is like unmixed polenta.

It is rather routine and not understanding which gives birth to habit.

The train stops in every station for people in love to find their pairs.

The drama of the Prince turned into a frog is that the rainy season's just begun.

When you run away from Happiness, in fact you run towards it.

I live on the ground floor of a skyscraper with glass lifts and mini-skirted lift operators.

I'm looking for a happy person to swap houses.

Tomorrow is the day you've been waiting for since today.

Any unhappiness is taken seriously by sadness.

During the dance of the bread the wheatears dance a hora.

To sing means giving voice to your soul.

If you are waiting for someone, don't press him/her.

Happiness is always after two unhappy souls.

You should live as desperately as you die
Or
Live and die desperately.

Everything that happens to us life is the shortest.

I love my Country although my passport has expired.

All my free days were on Sundays.

Young people cannot grow younger.

You cannot give what you have not, but you can receive.

Enemies hate you for your qualities, friends love you for your defects.

The mole loves the sun more than the sunflower does, but it is ashamed to tell it and show up.

True love lasts longer than intended.

The right of doing nothing was stipulated on a Sunday.

Sorrow overwhelms people faster than happiness.

Beauty is the nude wearing the right clothes size
Or
Beauty is the nude which has found the clothes that fit.

Success depends on public not on jury.

I am one of those people who would have starved to death if I hadn't had my soul with me.

Don't ask the doctor whether you have got well!

When you love someone, you also love what is not loveable about him/her.

When you love someone, you also love all their imperfections.

Ask God for everything and He will give you infinitely much more. Ask for nothing and He will give you His Kingdom.

Two-thirds of your enemies are present when your friends promise to support you.

Happiness is a poisoned gift. It has been given to mortals to make them regret life.

There is no such thing as a trip from where you don't come back spiritually richer than when you left.

If there is water between people in love, it can only be tears.

If snow falls, happiness cannot be far away.

They took/ate only one apple from Heaven.

Love needs love to resist.

There is a lot of expectation about something that never happens.

Adam and Eve didn't need a surname.

Can happiness and unhappiness fit together?

Mediocrity is as proud as democracy.

Keep on being famous although no one knows you!

So many flowers for just one spring...

All your enemies' chances used to belong to you.

If your happiness doesn't become universal, you don't deserve it.
Spring sees the flowers winter only dreams of.

If you achieve what you have planned, your achievement is modest.

We complain only in the name of something better.

Fortuitousness of Happiness is sporadic.

Perseverance is Glory attempt to get Eternity.

Waiting means slow hopes.

World vastity depends on the means of transport.

People tend to minimize the positive and exaggerate the negative aspects in a story.

When progress is profitable it no longer makes progress.

When a man is happy, his Guardian Angel is happier than him.

Rewarded heroism becomes heroic deed.

Love that wants peace still fights.

Greet everybody you meet before you succeed in getting on the underground.

Resting after a period of idleness makes you feel more tired.

Circle used to be the symbol of perfection before sphere.
Genius doesn't reject talent although it challenges it.

Swans come in winter; they are outnumbered by swallows in spring.

Will there be a shooting star for me when I end my life?

The happiness you share with the others is the boomerang of Peace.

A day doesn't begin when the night ends, but when you wake up.

Doors are for houses, gates for gardens and windows for souls.

The difference between an angel and a devil lies in our hopes not in the wings.

True love must pay bank instalments.

I think we belong to the Galaxy of Love, where the stars light not only their ways when they travel to each other, but they also give us a chance to catch a glimpse of our souls ignited by them.

If I managed to smile, I would take a selfie.

Love is what you feel when you feel everything.

To stop loving is like giving up living while you're still alive.

When you love you must love in earnest, when you hate you must pretend.

If Love and Lie compete, they both won.

The After Life World must be large indeed, since all of us go there and none of us comes back for lack of vacancies.

I love all my enemies, but I some of them are my favourites.

I have been alone all my life and now I can't help it.

One in one thousand marriage proposals is accepted. I am telling it from my personal experience.

Your personality may play tricks in you. I stopped talking to those who don't give me likes.

Life is earnest money given to mortals for the After Life.

If you turn round, you'll have bad luck. If you keep going forward, you'll reach the destination, but you'll miss something you need.

No happiness is yours, before you live it.

You also need a little happiness to feel better.

Cranes have come back but my soul is still there.

Have you noticed how soon the day breaks?
It happens overnight.

Today is a day you generally forget because it is only today.

Even a Destiny that goes against Life is worth living.

If you don't give in too easily, you amplify the conqueror's satisfaction.

Happiness is more dramatic if it happens.

I'm the angel no one wants as a guardian.

I've failed all my despairs.

There must be something true in what you remember.

It isn't polite to ask a woman her age. You can see it when she takes off her clothes.

I live in a ruinous castle. I can only make love on Mondays when the castle is not visited.

Compared to love, a kiss seems frivolous.

If you love, you may make someone fall in love with you.

Eternity is longer than the time allotted to it.

It is no use drinking together with those you get on well.

Every time we are defeated, we think it is a childhood game.

If you have money, you should spend it, if you don't, save it.

Make them want you and not wait for you!

I still haven't answered to the questions I was asked when I was in school.

The angels who guard the sinners are better- paid.

Love's echo is reflected back in two hearts.

Being alone is benefical only in the register of tenants.

Patience is the best hostess of success.

Doing nothing is not a way of waiting, but of postponing.

Future doesn't lie in front of us. It lies in our mind.

Success is partial if it doesn't change hierarchy.

After a victory, a loser is more tired.

Clothes worn indoors are totally indebted to changeable fashion.

Destiny is a scenario suggested by Gods.

Longing is the same, pain is always different.

Love forgives Happiness.

Any waiting is eternal.

Eternity is the second of grace.

Destiny is a scenario suggested by Gods.

While still an apprentice of love it is more important to learn how to wipe the lipstick off you than how to kiss.

If people had wings, they would be birds of prey, not angels.

Fashion is to Art what Spring is to Year.

Success is more about its length of time than its magnitude.

Any waiting is eternal.

Love forgives Happiness.

Destiny is a scenario suggested by Gods.

Clothes worn indoors are totally indebted to changeable fashion.

After a victory, a loser is more tired.

Happiness is a poisoned gift. It has been given to mortals to make them regret life.

It took me a day to tell you how little I have lived.

True heroes can be recognized by their wounds. The others by the badges.

We would expire so fast if all our life were worth living.

It is always great, after any victory, to come back to your village.

Have you ever met happy people who were hungry?

I have never had surface loves. All my dates have been in an underground station.

Destiny is shrewd: it places its stake on our life.

The World's beauty does not depend on aestheticians' evaluation.

The Devil complains about the Saints' privileges.

Be happy for someone else's happiness, if you want to partake in it.

Patience wins the race and loses all fans.

Beatitudes that don't come from Heaven don't touch the Earth.

The money you loan from a bank is yours.

Not only do I feel I'm a winner, but I'm also convinced.

Soul is the only island where all outcasts are welcome.

Soul is its own light.

God would have left me alone If the Devil hadn't tried to tempt me.

Village is soul that has found itself.

I was asked to be happy to no avail since it was not my girlfriend who did it.

We keep our Happiness behind the door, where we hide our sweetheart.

Thank God I am fond of you, otherwise you would be fond of me.

If love kept its word, it would become ridiculous.

A flower cannot hide a woman's face. It only replaces it.

Happiness, don't drop me from your claws!

Parents are our most recent history.

All truths have disappointed me.

Your look is not indecent, only what you're looking at.

I was asked to be happy to no avail since it was not my girlfriend who did it.

People have an expectation even from something that doesn't happen.

It is not enough for people to make peace, their ideas should join, too.

In vain do people make peace if their ideas do not join them.

Maids of honour are more experienced than the bride.

I've tested my lovers' memory and none of them remembers when I cheated on her for the first time.

You don't understand what happiness is if you can enjoy it till the end.

Those who are admitted in Heaven fire their Guardian Angels.

Idleness improves efficacy.

Subconsciousness works better than consciousness.

If you give me a day of happiness, I'll offer all the others to you.

Memories' snows fall, but they don't cover the ground.

Longing is the necessity of presence.

Happiness is the simultaneity of smiles.

Let yourself be carried by the wave that moves away from the shore!

We are sentenced to love each other, or else we risk becoming friends.
Don't take a risk with your first cards!

Spring has its weeds.

Half plus one represents majority only if they agree.

We depend on our Guardian Angel's presence/vigilance of mind.

All that is left for us is what hasn't happened yet.

I'm just one of those shadows that the sun only warms.

I comply to my freedom.
When one of the options enthrals you, you cannot say you have a choice.

One day is enough for you to understand how much you have lived.

The price of a ticket includes the ads, too.

Ads are included in the price of a ticket.

Loves never stay where you leave them.

If you do nothing you can get ill, but you don't if you do something you like.

Ia is our heart at its best.

I was never more optimistic than when I realized that all those people who didn't believe in me were wrong.

The bet you don't win at a gambling table is a project.

In life you smile more often in photos than under any other circumstances.

Every time I say I have a lot of friends I exaggerate. As a matter of fact, I don't know in whose favour.

After the wedding night, virginity is attributed to impotence.

In vain does he/she comes If you get bored waiting.

Rarely does celebrity lasts longer than the applauses.
If you can feel though your clothes, it means your clothes are modern.

When in front of you there is a precipice if you move forward, you make no progress.

We are most efficient in our spare time.

To be patient is like having money in your pocket while in an empty market.

The ignorant apply what they do not know more often than the wise do with what they have studied.

Love blown away by a typhoon needs just a soft breeze to be blown back.

Love your enemies, but don't betray your friends for them!

Future is like weather forecast: it comes true only on short term.

The Polar Star is helpless without favourable winds.

Happiness can deceive only the unhappy people.

Not so long ago it was enough for me to be happy in order to feel well.

Collective memory is the sum of individual amnesias.

Solitude is always present.

Loneliness is always present.

Nothing can be reduced to essence for it is in fact the enlarged detail.

Happiness has its own rules which make it impracticable.

The truth you cannot understand is deceiving.

You are always young in your memories and love.

What you ask from God ask for all your fellow people.

A failure which increases your will must be glorious.

A shadow is not related to the Sun but to the one who stand in its way.

If history didn't have heroes, it would be read only at the weekends.

The absent-minded people who don't turn back are not superstitious but proud.

Not only do victors make history, they also teach it to losers.

We are that kind of angels who are no longer satisfied with flight.

Silence is not short of words but courage.

Your life's eternity is the longest.
If the conductor had a good singing voice, he would join the choir.

Happiness put on weight when it was with me.

You do not take advantage of your free time if you do nothing.

We were born to be generous.

Mind forgets before soul can forgive.

Too many lipstick marks on icons.

We were born to be generous.

If your coming back journey does not take you home, it means you have moved out too many times.

We are birds of prey. Our nest is in the heart.

Pride's vanity is about giving up on everything that is uplifting.

Life is not accustomed to dying and therefore it takes sleeping lessons.

The nucleus is free, the electrons have only degrees of freedom.

Happiness asks for nothing and yet it is expensive.

Only when the sun is at zenith it does not cast shadows.

That is the rub -we have too much confidence in future.

Only on foot can you go from one happiness to the next one.

If it's cloudy, I double my optimism.

Even when nothing happens, it is wise to wait.

Life gives us much more trouble than food for thought.

It is easy to recognize envy since it applauds only its own success.

Hope can succeed without you, you cannot success without it.

You come back home not when you long for it, but when you only long for it.
Happiness lends. Sadness borrows forever.

I pestered the Saints till they gave me a coronet.

What would the fruit of magnolia tree be called if it had enough ambition?

Recollections are the memory's pride.

You cannot reduce truth to its content.

I have been told I am a walking encyclopaedia. Yes, it is true I like walking.

Not long ago my Destiny and I spied on each other.

How erotic the on-duty female student's mission sent to wet the sponge today sounds!

If you are given a choice, choose! If you aren't given a choice, refuse!

I didn't attend choir rehearsals because I was afraid of draughts.

When I was a kid and got lost on a beach, I was always found by a young lady I wanted to talk to.

Eternity is the period of time between a train you miss and the next one.

They say Victor Hugo had seventeen coitions per night.

This piece of information is more striking than his novels.

Future had nothing of interest for Nostradamus.

Love is the happiness that happens to two people.

Romanticism relies on incapacity of being a hero.

In kindergarten, I used to avoid eating my porridge, when the girls I used to kiss were present.

When nothing happens, everybody loses their patience.

It wouldn't be fair if I didn't defeat my enemies.
Notice in the forest: "No love -making in the wet areas".

Loving you realize how old you are.

Loving you realize your age.

Priests wouldn't read the newspapers if all those who confess their sins told the truth.

I am a hero as a matter of principle.

The definition of love can be found in a picture dictionary.

Keeping on loving you end up divorcing.

Happiness relies more on photos than on mirrors.

The girlfriend who feels content with just one kiss is not yours.

Who taught you to tell the truth, taught you to be a winner.

To be happy you must forget. To stay happy you must remember.

Happiness leaves barefoot footprints over those left by stiletto shoes.

I did not know how to be happy. The proof is that I was.

Happiness and sadness drag the same prey.

When you stop loving, all you can do is to love again.

Happiness is the sublime state of sadness.
That is why we cry when we are happy.

No matter how long it takes you to be happy, you still have enough time to get sad.

Happiness has always complained of staff shortage.

We try to be happy every second and when we succeed, we want to know why.

Happiness is like you are under water. You do not resist long.

We fail two thirds of our happiness. Our enemies help us with the rest.

There are so many people who pretend they are happy that you no longer know who to believe.

When aboard the plane you sit and fly. So do you when in love.

Trees don't have to smear their branches with ground to blossom.

At a certain time, Happiness becomes unbearable You must enjoy it by that time.

In railway stations flowers sell better than doughnuts.

Starting with a certain age any diminutive name you are called by, sounds ridiculous.

Love allows you to decide not to choose.

Everything which is above the knee long is modern.

Too much sun in the eyes too little in the hearts.

Don't underestimate your enemy's joke!

We can be happy in the six years spent at home before going to school.

Nostradamus was right: within a line one can foretell everything.

When your girlfriend takes off her clothes, you get a chill down your spine.

Cyprus dies on its own grave.

When you forgive, your soul is willing to love.

Such as our soul feels pain, so do the wings of the birds.

Soul's flowers must be plucked at night.

Mutual future requires mutual hopes.

Give up on your first love only if new ones are born.

Don't pay attention to minor enemies! The major ones don't let them defeat you.
At 20 you are young. Every ten years after, you are young again.

All rich relatives are long living.

What you ask God for is in devils' arms.

I have bought a ticket for a trip around the world, but the world is gone.

You may live on the seashore, but you still get thirsty.

Like a rabbit I jumped from one love to another. How prolific I am!

When you get a divorce, you think it will last.

I have never wished to be young, but to stay young.

I will have a flat as a memorial house.
Every time I wanted to get married, many people waited in a queue.

Whenever I wanted to get married there were too many people waiting in a line.

We love with our extremities.

I don't fall in love for principle. I fall in love for love.

We go to bed as if we are going to start working.

On top of all love does not last long...

The hair on a man' s chest is as much as a woman' pubic hair.

We always say we have enough time to pass away some other day.

I am a prophet hired only to forecast the weather.

I am not an age. I am a number of years.

Ant colonies avoid sunstroke due to my shadow.

I have taken my few words from silence.

I am an ill-mannered guy who knows how to apologize.

Even if I am giving you love it is still too little.

Dream-ineffective sleep.

I loved the stars not knowing that actually they were in the lake.

I haven't forgotten any of my girlfriends. All of them have forgotten me though.

A day should not pass just like that. Neither should a night.

Progress limit is success.

No day went by without my involvement.

If I had a place in an icon, it would be outside it.

I can anticipate what will happen to me. But after.

I was unfaithful to my mistresses with my wife.

Life's tragedy doesn't reside in its last moment, but in all the others.

How accurate envy is!

It takes me a whole day to get ready to go to bed.

I haven't found any phone number in Kamasutra.

Only for us, the earthlings, the moon is bigger than all the night stars.

No matter how beautiful a dream is, you are not sleepy because of it, but because you are tired.

As a bird cannot fly without its wings, neither can a man move further without hope.

Who waits for tomorrow does not deserve today.

A believer repents more than a sinner.

If you love, you will never love enough. Only hatred is infinite.

Snowdrops love snow more than they love spring.

When your wife says you have lost your stamina, your mistress suggests a massage.

Your parents are your first love.

Flowers cannot hide a woman's face. It is in them.

One can only love at night who he/she loved by day.

Not even a beautiful woman can make you love her.

Loves are so much alike. You don't even realize when you are unfaithful to them.

Nothing of what you love you leave behind at home.

Impotence doubles compliments.

The longer spring is, the more pathetic it is.

If people need happiness, sadness pushes them toward it.

In order for people to believe in God, the devil has to exist.

No condom is roomy enough when the woman is beautiful.

Life is a beautiful woman who makes you a child every day.

Truth is stronger than its defenders.

If the way a question is well conceived, the answer is suggested.

Love and agony in the same bed.

We pray to God, whereas the devil asks us.

Life is about demand and supply. We are in charge with supplying.

People who wear a watch unlike those who don't, know how long they are late.

In love nothing is done seriously.

We take horizon for what lies in front of us.

If you like a lie it may become the truth.

People are not afraid to tell lies, but they are afraid to tell the truth.

If a man leaves the room when his phone rings, he is called by his mistress. If he says he is having a meeting, he is called by his wife.

Of all the people who had a spite against me, not even one was my enemy.

Two free days in a row makes a weekend.

If you have forgiven someone you cannot hate them.

Everything you wished for is in your regrets.

You are closest to happiness when you don't wish for it. The main difference between an angel and a devil is not the absence of horns but the presence of wings.

But for the fashion, we would not be in love with the same person.

They don't teach happiness at school. It only happens when one of your teachers is in love with his/her subject.

In statistics the error is in calculating the mean.

I have loved all **my girlfriends.** It explains my failures.

Life is a wake where people tittle tattle.

A registry officer was once asked by a couple whether they had to dress as bride and groom for the divorce

Don't be upset you have lost the key, you still have the house.

A man whose cheeks are red when he comes out a woman's bedroom, has either been slapped or made love to her.

Cobra venom is the only potion that cooled down Cleopatra's hot blood.

Nefertiti, the only swan that didn't migrate from Egypt.

I have failed my career. I should have become either a doctor or a writer.

The Earth is looking for a planet which doesn't depend on electricity.

Don't tell people you are happy, or else they will make you believe otherwise.

Doctors only delay your meeting with God.

I haven't loved naked women.

A barometer turns upside down in the vaginal area.

Giovanni Boccaccio loved in time of plague, Gabriel Garcia Marquez in time of cholera. What would they have done in time of covid pandemic?

I've forgotten all the lessons taught at school but none of my loves.

A kiss consists of all love words in all spoken languages.

I used to be a mere human before I discovered love.

Success moves ahead, glory upwards.

If loves kept their word, our lives would be predictable.

The rhymed Cioran is the second Eminescu.

I am a flower at a zoo.

Any time you make love you deflower.

Happiness and sadness counter clockwise face the same problem-duration.

For my enemies' sake I bear happiness.

When you love your dormant corpse in your body, is resuscitated.

If drones made honey, they would no longer be interested in queen bees.

After all we live in the idealized world of our forefathers.

If Hemingway and Fitzgerald' s generation was a lost one, what is ours like?

Kamasutra is read faster in two.

Failure is not when someone else fails, but when you fail.

God has given people everything but faith in Him. They must get it on their own.

My problem is not that I don't have talent, but that I am not aware I don't.

A memory stick of my works will be laid next to Eminescu's manuscripts sometime in the future.

I am more self-confident when I make a mistake.

I have given my mother so many daughters -in -law that she should have had dozens of grandchildren.

I am so tired that even my annual leave exhausts me.

If you love spring, it means you have never got drunk.

A hope told becomes a lamentation.

The last year grapes are about to ripe.

This year I have been ill twice and have had a cold head once.

I have cried so much that should have bought a water meter.

A good doctor, just like a good mentor, teaches you how to outlive him/her.

Of love take only as much you need and leave some for the others.

If you don't know how to love, your soul will teach you.

Only the heart in which blood flows is alive.

I didn't say goodbye to you because I have never left you.

Don't love your enemy only because you are afraid of him/her.

I have taken a day-off of my Sundays.
I was unfaithful to my mistresses with my wife.

Life's tragedy doesn't reside in its last moment, but in all the others.

How accurate envy is!

It takes me a whole day to get ready to go to bed.

I have one thousand thoughts and none of them agrees with me.

Lies must be explained, truth is demonstrated.

I went in the forest to listen to the birds. But they were listening to each other.

I cook in my free time and when I start to work, I eat.

At an age when I could have been happy, I had all childhood illnesses.

Although Lucifer had wings, he fell to the ground. This was the first lesson of flight.

Freud justified Kamasutra.

Aristotle philosophised while walking. Kant walked after.

Decency is the feminine shame.
Memory is the mind's ballast. For a while it keeps it floating but, in the end, it sinks it.

If God saw to all the prayers, the Saints would be out of work.

Truth allows to be contested to make followers.

Apocalypse is when people are late, and trains arrive in time.

Certainties are revised opinions.

Typos minimize the authors' grammatical gaps.

The more prestigious the world gets, the less charming.

Suicide has in it something reminding of a vaudeville.

To reduce yourself to essential is to increase yourself.

Homer was spared of love at first sight.

Patience was the bait used by Chronos to fool his fans.

A mirror and a portrait flatten the face- the supreme form of distortion.

Dogs on a leash have a more vicious bite.

Hope is the figure of speech for will.

Like any happy emperor I need several flies.

It is enough to be happy to be right.

Chronos said to his son Zeus, pointing to some patient people: "I will rule over these people, the others are yours"

Jealousy puts on yellow clothes, but it can't stand the red ones.

Long time ago truth was verified by reductio ad absurdum. At present lie is validated like that.

There are fallen angels, but no fallen Saints. He who has experienced the falling of his country people, avoid it as an individual.

When you are lying down your **horizon is limited**.

Love the women detested by the others and you will end up loving all of them.

Life is like going ziplining. By the time you come to its end you have the feeling you die thousands of times.

What love forgets, jealousy remembers.

Memory condemns us to repetition. Innovation is amnesic.

Joy is practical happiness.

Nowadays Freud's sofa has been remodelled.

Love is sentimental progress.
If you come back on the same route, you'd better stay where you have arrived.

Night has a shadow, day has thousands.

Eternity is the time God has chosen for Himself.

During an investigation initiated by Sherlock Holmes, Sir Arthur Conan Doyle imagined a titanic endeavour, that of copying by hand all the volumes of Encyclopaedia Britannica, the perfect alibi to dig a gallery leading to the Bank of London, to its gold ingots. I can't help shuddering and asking myself what could be behind each work.

I am John Keats' twin brother. I was so close to have talent.

The only truths are those everybody is interested in. The rest is gossip.

Happiness is the failure sadness knows about, but it is proud of it.

A married woman is not a picked flower. It is a flower which will bear fruit out of admiration.

No one takes our despairs seriously. Not even the psychiatrist we pay to do it.

Sweat is blood that no longer wants to impress with its colour.

Beggars lend money to each other, the rich don't.

Love fools you twice: at the beginning when you believe you are in love, and at the end when you believe you are out of it.

When you lose patience, be careful, you should be on your own.

A mistress could replace ten wives, but she wouldn't be like any of them.

Women are able to schedule even their monthly periods. Men are unpredictable.

What I love about women, I detest about men.

You cannot survive if you don't love life.

Affection is the cat of love.

Stations are the only places where we are impudent enough to wait in public.

There are still plenty of daisies in the field. After all my love may come.
Proud people don't love, they want to be loved.

Love's quarantine is shorter than the incubation period for any venereal diseases.

If you are not sincere, you can tell any woman you love her.

Gods incite Chronos against us.

Seeing the sand in the sandglass Chronos realizes how little people understand what he does.

If you can forgive a traitor, he/she has done something to your advantage.

Weather forecasters don't make plans for longer than three days.

Scholars study extra-terrestrial signals. I cannot understand my girlfriend's either.

Love is a lily. It makes you feel dizzy if you sleep with it at night.

All heroines disguise themselves as men.

Doctrine is an embalmed idea.

A wingless bird continues being free only if the desire to be free is born in it.

Forgetfulness is the virtue for an avenger.

I am carrying my thoughts in my minds like the Holy Relics in a silver reliquary.

The truth is the error in the scholars' heads.

At the very first Spanish lesson you understand that in the language of "Don Quixote", the verb "haber" has nothing to do with possession.

Jesus Christ's tomb was guarded by some Roman soldiers. The Agony on the Cross made them suspicious.

Parents take you out of childhood, grandparents take you back there.

The tomb which permanently has fresh flowers is the richest.

A fly can drive crazy even a military strategist.

Even happy people hope in a better destiny.

Glory disturbs creation. It must be posthumous. They applaud only at the end of an opera.

If you keep on saying you will die, one day you will become a prophet.

Visionaries do not think highly of present time.

God is lenient to those who confess their sins. That explains why sinners are talkative.

Women succeed where men fail. Men call it "chance."

Oysters are eaten raw. Otherwise, they will be icky

Actually, time does not pass. It only makes us believe it does, to increase memories ad infinitum.

God banished us from Heaven, but He left the Gates open.

We abandoned the idea of flight before our wings grew.

God loves us not to love Him back but to love each other.

God created the world out of nothing but to create the man He needed some matter.

There are two ways you can take someone else's guilt over you: by forgiving or by taking revenge. Only the former is moral.

If chess had been played with dice too, it would have been more like real life.

Like a moth I take pleasure in women's clothes.

Love was given to us not to be happy, but to be.

On Sundays God makes us work for Him.

Expectations are more boring when they come true.

History offers the past a future.

How inspired I was to be happy!

How easily we trade life in exchange for a few hours of sleep every night.

Smile replaces laughter when thought replaces affect.

Memory is the effort of not forgetting.

Loneliness is the gift that- sadness offers to us in exchange for anxiety.

To allows being loved is to allow being cheated.

Night wants us asleep so it can wear its stars in peace.

You regret only what has happened to you with your consent.

When you forgive out of love you also find excuses.

Most teachers are generous when they mark their students to prove how effective their teaching methods are.

Modesty is such a rare trait that those who have it must be proud of it.

Exaggeration is nothing but putting it bluntly with capital letters.

When traitors find themselves among winners, they are taken for plants among losers.

There is so little truth in exposed love.

Give love the kiss you expect from it.

Mornings begin the moment you wake up.

We make mistakes only in the name of an illusion.

Demands are not big if they are yours.

As Hell was close to Heaven, the former had to shrink.

I help only those who accept to owe me.

In vain did the fish caught in a net. avoid the bait in the rod hook.

The umbrella I left behind in the underground, is he I found in the park.

The Angel is the Saint whom God didn't consider capable of becoming a Man.

When it is about Man, both God and the devil have expectations.

When a husband takes a mistress, his wife starts wearing mini.

You are generous indeed, not if you give, but if you refuse to receive.

A dream is that part of sleep which is not taxed.

Sadness relies on memories, happiness in hopes.

People feel tempted to say "I love you" every time they make love. Atavism of initial sincerity.

When a sinner confesses his/her sins, he/she says the same things he/she says when he/she prays.

Jealousy begins with impotence.

The truth told to your friends is gossip, the truth told to your enemies is martyrdom.

Fata Morgana is thought to be an optical illusion. Actually, it is a spiritual illusion.

Lipstick makes lips talk.

Some pirates attacked a ship. They asked for gold. As they were not given, they asked for booze. As they were not given, they asked for women. As they were not given, they left Ko.

Let's not be afraid of the ending, but of the beginning that will not continue.

A woman makes you intoxicated more than an entire grapevine.

Unhappy people have comparative memory.

A lie can be more credible than truth.

Great literature expands time. Siglo de Oro the Spanish Golden Century, lasted for two centuries, the sixteenth and seventeenth.

The sun can be found in bread, which the wheat ears don't keep only for them.

The only thing you can snatch from happiness is its memory.

After a defeat you need two victories to recover.

Without sacrifice heroes would be simply lucky.

Always wait sides with those who are not in a hurry.

If I had met Yogi Berra, he would have taught me basketball and nothing else.

When naked your mistress looks like your wife.

I know how to defend myself, but I don't know against whom.

You mustn't trample the grass, not even when you are barefoot.

The book saves us from the evil outside it.

Snails and lovers are in love with the rain, The former leave their homes, the latter go in.

Happiness changes a chuckle into a smile.

Voluptuousness always wears a small size.

Happy experiences do not get along with each other.

Silence is the shroud spread over the words.

Don't ask life for a day off. It may misunderstand you and give you Death.

Heart is a drum which sounds louder when someone else strikes it.

It's useless writing what the others wrote. To do it you must read all of them.

Happiness is the optimal way of wasting your time.
One thousand happy people cannot understand one single sad person.

The moonrise and the moonset are as spectacular as the sun, but nobody admires them.

Future's bad luck is that not everybody has the chance to live it.

You can blame happiness for many things.

Decency was born when men took off their hats because of the heat.

Never forget your friends, particularly if you have lent them some money!

Sinners think God is watching them to punish them at the last judgement.

Wrinkles are like dress pleats: they don't have to be fashionable, but chic.

School paradox: teaches' mistakes can have good results if they are successfully applied by students.

Ignorance is to unimportant things what predisposition is to important things.

The day's fertility is waiting for its clouds.

No one can postpone their destiny beyond the due moment when it must take place.

The neuter countries have won all the wars.

Shyness covers my soul like quills cover a hedgehog's back. One can cares me only on my belly.

We are alike only when naked. It explains the success of fashion.

When you love you also love what you don't like.

Siesta joy exceeds the appetite.

After eating, the rich thank the chef whereas the poor thank God.

The devil takes God's favourite space.

The purest air in Europe is in Calabria. Therefore, Fata Morgana is often seen there.

Smile is the beauty of the lips.

I told Death: "As you have come, will stay with me till the wake begins?"

I have a high opinion of the devils: I think they are contemporary with Angels.

Some foes brought to my attention the fact that I am a hero.

"You learn how to be a good bricklayer working high on the scaffolding" The senior mason told me pushing me off it.

I am sadder than dead people. Unlike them I haven't met death.

I was nor born because I was due. I was born because my mother was nine months pregnant.

My mother held fast to religious traditions, and I held her hand.

I was the first to realize I was immortal, and all the others imitated me.

Memory is a blotter which absorbs all the facts but afterwards everything is illegible.

To Nico: Summer lets its long hair loose over the Sun's shadow.

If you don't know who to blame, you blame yourself.

Futurologists are the only historians you cannot contradict.

Fiction books should be like playing cards: as few signs as possible and more and more imagination.

Without an umbrella even a summer shower seems long.

Our hopes are like tree leaves: their only purpose is to feed us for a while.

It is alright if you wake up with a pessimistic thought.

You have enough time to forget it.

You make the most enemies after you pass away.

Platonic love is a term invented by Plato's whistle-blowers.

The term computer is outdated. Today computers compute nothing.

Beauty bears false witness in the spiritual love court trial.

Love is like gold in a mine: hard to extract and full of impurities.

Forgetfulness is involuntary forgiveness.

A bed is a love altar on condition the sacrifice is hot.

A friend stays by your side till you succeed, an enemy till you fail.

A bad begun day is going to be long.

Judging them by their breasts, women should have two hearts.

Any sleeping slave is free.

Whoever reduces everything to essential, loses the rest.

School teachers teach us how to write only to have what to correct later.
But for Shakespeare, only matinee plays would have been performed.

Everything that can turn humans into gods is progress.

A weekend when you get bored is the same as a working day.

It is difficult to prove one's love without having children.

Everything I know about shame was taught to me in the first form.

Several more centuries of culture and we will come back to Renaissance.

A woman's nakedness is like the surface of water. Even sailors can drown because of it.

In their own special way even your best friends have your best interest at heart.

We are like whales. No matter how much water we have, we still don't have enough air

On a chessboard the bishop has the largest room for manoeuvre.

You learn the first foreign language when you learn how to tell the truth.

The moment you get bored eternity begins.

Mini skirts make you bend down very low.

A unicorn is just the Apis's Bull despair to run faster, losing a horn.

I have counted neither my ex-girlfriends nor the books I have written since they are the same.

The Sun and the Moon aren't alike only at noon.

In Newton's Era, Einstein would have been a Newton.

Just like the Sirens who sing because they suffer from seasick, I write because I suffer from this world sick.

God asks from you what you cannot give Him to see whether you are gullible enough to try it. This is Faith.

I am like Aristotle and Descartes: nothing of what I say is true, but I cannot be contradicted.

Nowadays the balcony scene from 'Romeo and Juliet' takes place in a lift.
I have spent the summer on my own together with a couple of cherries.

The ambition you don't forget, turns into will.

The caterpillar is the butterfly's repentance.

A panther abandons her cub only if the latter eats more than her.

Nothing in more fruitful for the soul than an unfulfilled hope.

Hope is the rational argument through which an optimist tries to convince a pessimist.

I'll be waiting for you as long as you want, but not a moment longer.

Everything you fail, you fail because you haven't tried enough times.

If the Destiny is repeated/repeats itself, it is enough for it to become ordinary/banal/commonplace.

The mistress has all the pretentions the wife has, but she expresses them in bed.

The seeds of glory don't bear fruit if the land is not worked.

The past is the accomplice of the future.

Happiness is the progress of joy without the help of technology.

Silence is the appropriate answer to an unasked question.

A nymphomaniac goes to the seamstress just to have her measures taken.

In culture, ecumenism means reading Shakespeare in Hindi.
Past is the only tense Memory can conjugate.

The lying witness prefers to be the last to speak.

Death always amazes us: it stiffens and dumbfounds us.

Destiny gives you less than you wish for, but more than it intended initially.

An ethics book is like a cookery book: it doesn't help you if you have no kitchen.

It is not true that the big fish swallows the small fish. If it were true, there would be only one big fish in an aquarium.

Children tell the truth, but not when it is about a missing cake.

In autumn I make dew people and leave them in the fields for winter.

Nothing else makes you look old like failed youth.

Happiness is soul's thirsty state looking for eternal elixirs.

When the Truth clears its throat, the Lie starts coughing.

I've looked over market price- list, I'll buy it.

If whales were not afraid, they might overturn our vessels, they would be as playful as dolphins.

Knees are nor for walking forward, but for praying.

If a woman is nine months late, no need for you to wait for her.

Any Paradise you can be banished from, should not be regretted.

When I told a fortune teller what I dream, he told me to stop falling asleep while watching TV.

To compensate human's sadness, he was given a permanent mating state period.

Breasts swell (charge up) even when they don't lactate.

Pay attention to what weather forecasters say, take your umbrella just in case.

Frogs talk to the clouds about the rain.

Time is life's baking powder.

Today is when present time is being introduced.

A question has to wait longer for its answer than the other way around.

Announcement: Sperm donor in a woman's receptacle.

Happenstance is more determining than destiny.

Even the best actors cannot walk on a wire that is not perfectly stretched.

The gift of singing was given to a bird when it was given the gift of flight.

Even a fakir considers empty plastic bottles more dangerous than shards.

Memory bothers only those people who have memories.

During a fasting period even the monks dream about sausages.

Wait only for what you have promised yourself.

**The sleepwalker avoids insomnia.**

Life is the failure of existence.

If we were perfect, we would no longer need God, the Craftsman who premeditated his rejects.

All angiosperms take the risk and bloom. All carnivorous plants take advantage of them.

Human's involution started the moment he thought himself a God.

If you pray to God when some others are present, you do not pray to Him.

A nightmare is awakening from a dream.

A man who loves himself has a perception problem.

Exile is the country where they ask for your passport to see who you are. At home, they ask for your identity card.

The earlier institutional education starts the more years they steal from your good family upbringing.

Death is committing suicide when God witnesses it/ in God's presence/in God's company.

Patience minimizes hope.

Aphrodite spread aphrodisiacs while Venus spread venereal diseases. This is the difference between Greek culture and Roman pragmatism.

If when you invite a woman to dance you think about what comes next, you should choose a symphony.

Sighing brings the most oxygen to the brain.

Emil Cioran used to talk for hours on the phone about his cold head to Virgil Ierunca. I wonder what dissertations he would have done if he had been contemporary with Covid 19.

A blood-stained flag even if it is on the ground it is hoisted.

When a thief meets another thief, he/she tries to steal his/her skeleton key.

Children play with the butterflies and parents kill the caterpillars.

A beautiful woman opens the door smiling and closes it talking.

He who predicts other people's future, cannot predict his own.

When we are naked, the Moon still keeps a cloud veil.

Don't trust the friend who has other enemies than you have.

Today computers compute nothing.

Beauty bears false witness in the spiritual love court trial.

If you don't know who to blame, you blame yourself.

Futurologists are the only historians you cannot contradict.

Fiction books should be like playing cards: as few signs as possible and the more and more imagination.

Without an umbrella even a summer shower seems long.

Our hopes are like tree leaves: their only purpose is to feed us for a while.

It is alright if you wake up with a pessimistic thought. You have **enough time to forget** it.

You make the most enemies after you pass away.

If you are as old as in your ID card you are old indeed.

**Platonic love is a term invented by Plato's whistle-blowers.**

People/Humans imagined an Almighty God not to obey Him, but to have their sins forgiven.

Of all Greek heroes, I detest Bellerophon most because he killed Chimera.

Whenever I see a beautiful woman barefoot, I imagine her wearing high heels.

When you thrust a knife in a loaf of bread you don't kill it.

Weightlessness is perceived only in bed and in outer space.

A bed covered in silk is more rustling than a forest in autumn.

The less we sleep in a bed the larger it is.

I feel more at ease when I lose than when I win.

Between Heaven and Earht, what could Jesus ascending and Lucifer descending have told each other?

No invention hurt Human so much like Time…

"Salt to Food" is a tale written by a hypertensive individual.
The mistress finds fleas in the conjugal bed.

Heaven is populated with many devils, too. Lucifer is only the fallen one.

Leaves fall only where they find a lake to float on.

A pillow is a cushioned falling out of dreams.

To wait for progress is to deny it.

An angel concerned with the tiara loses his/her wings
Saints are angels with sexual dimorphism.

Gratitude is more than love. It is its sacrifice in order to make its way back on the thorny road of memories.

Death is more relaxed than Life. It has all the time in the world on its side.

In vain do you ask God for forgiveness if you did wrong to people.

A nursing mother has milk for all the children in a village, a mother doesn't have enough for her own.

If you cannot swim, you can drown in salt water.

Freedom is the implementation of passion.

It is difficult to find the path if you are alone in the forest.

A child born on the other side of the blanket eats on loan.

If you break the piggy bank, you lose the money that was in it, too.

While living you meet with temptations.

Love poems are handwritten.

Hair is the adornment that a face wears every day.

If you have no question to ask, you haven't understood.

Who hasn't learnt how to relax in water, cannot swim /doesn't know how to swim.

A deed that must/is to be justified is corrupt.

In times of drought the thorns of a cactus get sharper.

Ambitions are thousands, will is only one.

As the rainbow cannot decide on a particular colour, it chooses its beauty.

The truth someone tells you is like the water they drink, telling you it is good.

A tigress that leaves its cub in the thicket of the trees doesn't abandons it, it leaves it to be protected by the forest.

**On your way to virtue, you meet temptation.**

No future is more promising than a past you haven't lived.

People remember best a sin which is not theirs: the Original Sin.

If you don't feel the need to be happy again, it means you have never been.

A beautifully dressed woman wants to lure you. When she is naked, she won't let you go.

A woman is like an onion: the more clothes you remove off her, the more emotional you become.

Beauty is like summer heat: it persists during the night, too.

What comes from your heart is called love.

The confessed sin equally redeems you from the good deed you keep secret.

A rose has more thorns than petals.

When cuddled even a black cat can bring good luck.

When a flower is picked it gives off its fragrance on your hands. The one which is not picked, slips it into your soul.

People who appreciate the song of the birds keep them in cages. Those who love them set them free.

Life is a cerement, a crumpled shroud, which we have all the time in the world to flatten.

A happy man and an unhappy man do the same things, but the former does them enthusiastically.

God gives you your friends, while the devil gives you your enemies. The latter is more generous.

If you give away to someone who begs outside a church, you give away to God who wants to help you.

I read only the books whose foreword I write.

Lucifer says God has pushed him.

Autumn comes only to flower what has not flowered.

Happy people have no master.

The eagles drop the eggs off the cliffs in order to break them open, but they are very patient with the eggs in their nest.

The less educated the parents are, the more convinced they are that their children are very successful.

Up to a certain age one of the two partners in a couple switches off the light when they make love not to be seen. Then after a certain age they do it not to see each other.

On the road to Happiness the post signs guide you in the opposite direction.

Long journeys don't always take you farther. / Long roads don't always take you far.

The road is the apparition of the horizon.

A road that leaves behind only dust doesn't deserve to be taken.

No one else can decide in your name not even you.

Theology and Science make the same mistake: they try to find logic and meaning in a world created out of chaos.

Autumn smells of love and quinces.

Autumn barricades itself in the attics among the leaves of dried grass and King Apples.

An umbrella keeps the rain, but not the clouds away.

An umbrella protects you from the rain, but not from the clouds.

Smiling is telling the truth unintentionally.

When a song is being sung, it is no longer true.

Your enemies are more like you than your friends.

Enemies represent you better than friends.

If you tell the truth, you don't need a mike.

Whoever tells the truth does not need a microphone.

People have invented time only because the medallions on their bracelets were dull.

Osier willow gets heavier after death.

Osier willow holds more weight after death than when it is alive.

The best reward for a job done is a pensive rest.

When I lose I am calmer than when I win.

It is not glory you should give up on, but its kudos.

Only lessons taught at the right time are not forgotten/ are remembered/ are kept in mind.

Who is happy in solitude, is not alone.

Time future is time present we keep on postponing for fear of time past.

Someone who works is more patient than someone who does nothing.

If you work, you are more patient than someone who does nothing.

The more pillows you sleep on the more illusive your sleep is.

Dreamers need pillows by day, too.

No matter how much I reproach my enemies with, I admit they have always been close to me.

Lie stays away from truth just like shadow stays away from sunshine.

People who say you are right when you are wrong are not your friends.

Autumn pale leaves are more sincere than spring multi-coloured flowers.

In the name of love you can fail, but you are not supposed to lie.

FOR NICO Nothing compares to happiness, not even living it.

For Marius Musat: Clothes are Angels' plumage.
Fashion is Angels' plumage.
Clothing is Angels' plumage.

New Year always starts between two others.

Lord, I'll love my enemies, but let me start with my female enemies!

When you smile you let the truth out of the bag.

When you smile you tell the truth unwittingly.

Waiting for progress is denying it.

Lucifer says God has pushed him.

God gives you friends, the devil gives you enemies. The latter is more generous.

If you meet someone begging outside a church, they are God who wants to help you.

The years when you were not happy cannot be reimbursed.

Even the shadow of a flower is scented.

The dog is that friend who doesn't bark when you are happy.

A contemplating eye cannot weigh.

Thinking is my habit.

The only illness that is yours is incurable.

If you live long, it is time's credit.

If you live a useful life, it is a gift of your soul.

Jesus baptized his soles by walking on water.

He who loves himself hugs himself. When his hands are around his body- he cannot do anything else.

God does not want us to suffer. He just wants us to know that pain exists.

Every time we lose blood from our heart, it makes room for our soul.

We have to choose between dirt and dust because we are proud.

Respect is harsh adoration.

Martyrs do not die. They are killed.

If God wants, man has only to ask.

Who is speaking about miracles has angel wings for rent.

The padlock that locks your wealth deposit can lock your soul, too.

The dissention between Churches strengthens the sects.

By definition love is about forgiveness.

The appeal to Last Inquest refers to the sentence, not to its duration.

I will sacrifice myself. That is all I can do under the circumstances.

Let me die! It is my spare time.

"How nice my shadow is!", the pygmy said appreciatively.

We start watching our life when we are old.

The semantron is the heart that beats in churches.

Crying because of a memory is like laughing at what is going to happen.

The vessel of faith, either broken or cracked, still leaks.

No matter how much we weigh, in Heaven we are weightless.

If you keep waiting for someone who is waiting for you, you will never meet them.

When you are happy, you no longer know who makes you happy.

When Catechism had the answers, they had to decide upon the questions people could have asked.

I want nothing. That is what I want.

On your way to the church there are a lot of temptations, on your way back home there are none.

The water flows fast in the Valley of Longing.

When we are anointed, our body becomes like the body of a fish. We are taken to all the aerial toll houses.

Who burdens your income, does not settle your risk.

Death doesn't only get to the dying man.

Good luck is like the fish that jumps onto your boat. If you don't catch it, it jumps back into the water.

Fear is useless. We do not fear what has happened but what might happen to us.

As the fruit is on the table, so is Faith; it is there, or it is not. And, when it is, it's total.

People's capacity of knowing God is related to their capacity of knowing themselves.

The sacrifice God asks from us is smaller than the sacrifice we ask from Him.

While in a church, just like Jesus, you may stand next to a robber. You will not become a robber yourself, but you can save him/her.

God's strength is love. Our weakness is hatred.
Only heartless people are ugly.

Nothing eternal can be measured.

In the rich man's golden watch there are as many minutes as there are in the poor man's copper watch.

The evidence that God has risen, is the fact that the oil they used to anoint His legs, is now the myrrh on our foreheads.

In order to point at you, you are first hit with the stone they are holding in their hands.

The Devil clings to the angel's wings not because he wants to fly, but because he wants them to pull themselves close.

There is as much Truth as there is Faith.

Light sins are more tempting for the hypocrites.

Healthy people may get ill, too.

A man's capacity of understanding depends on their ability of imagining.

Who ignores God's words, has not heard them.

Who dies first, does not go to Heaven by all means.

Our tomb stone becomes the church above us, and we will ascend to Heaven through it.

Who is happy to do a good deed helps twice.

Kneecaps, the sesamoid bones, are the seeds of our knees that make the land fertile, when we kneel down to pray.

Don't ask God for something you are unworthy of, for if He gives it to you, you will disgrace yourself.

The way to God is vertical. You cannot go on foot, you need wings.

The sky is much, much higher than we are. This should be the dimension of our humbleness, too.

We find excuses for our mistakes, pointing out some others, more serious, that we have avoided.

We do not ask questions because we are afraid of answers.

Faith and health are more about what we should do and less about what we do.

Life is prison-breaking. No matter how far you get at a certain moment, they will catch you.

Grace is Beauty that ignores itself.

Aesthetics is women's mythology.

"My Lord, guide us along your righteous way!"

Don't hurry to know, for those who know, forget. Strive to understand, for those who understand, take action.

In a wicked world, Good stands out effortless, like a flower among weeds. It is a pity not to do it.

People that do not understand what justice is, take the law into their own hands.

Jesus was the Teacher who selected His Apprentices. Today students choose their teachers.

Make mistakes every day! Don't make them every hour!

Life is a fight. The more personal it is the more peaceful you are.

God has all our thoughts in His thought. Descartes's saying "I think, therefore I am" is in fact "I think therefore I am in God."

The world is good, but there is no more room for us in its goodness.

God knows our sins. Confession helps us to admit them and repent for them.

If a man asks you for something, ask him to forgive you for not having noticed his poverty.

Life is a cage. If we have not come across its iron bars, we have not run far enough.

Who can teach me what leaving is, better than those who are coming back?

Oblivion is the only way of forgiving.

If the Devil is your travel companion, then the journey is short.

If you die, you have all the chances to come back to life. If you live, you have all the chances to die.

Alienation is when you stop pushing yourself hard enough. Solitude is when you have found yourself.

You can leave for lots of destinations. You come back from only one of them.

Doubt is not the denial of faith, it is its confirmation.

When a storm takes place in us, it turns into a drizzle that brings about rich crops.

Only a few hours of sleep separates dream from reality.

If you cease looking for your completion, after you have found it, it signals out you have come across someone else's.

Unannounced comings are not biblical.

The parsimony of abeyance: "someone may come."

The gods have locked me in a cave that has too many exists so as to have me their permanent prisoner.

The gift is never given back. You have to make the best use of it.

"Tomorrow will I be as good as I am today?" -it is a question asked by a weightlifter not a hermit.

It is not the journey that is important, but the direction.

Body without soul is nothing as is The Earth without the Sun.

The most fertile land belongs to the body.

There are people who can keep their promises only if they tell lies.

Only those who do not understand their fault break free.

A bird can fly effortlessly both over high and low mountains.

When we die, we are replaced by the best actions we did.

Who is afraid of death, has never raised their eyes to Heaven.

People have the feeling they are united because they are many.

An animal in pain, if provoked, becomes a worse animal. A man in pain becomes a better person.

Memories capitalize on the past. Memoires account for it.

Who takes the law into their own hands shares the guilt with the culprit.

Soul is a lordly game. Its bones shouldn't be left on the tray.

Don't smile! Keep your hair on!

By forgetting your duties, you already get some more.

In a moving world those who stand still, regress.

We look for happiness, although the Bible includes verses about happiness.

Life has given everything to me. I have given the rest of it to it.

Impartiality separates the world's halves.

Come, my love! Your health is up to me.

Stars - the tear drops on the night's face – are falling one by one into the sea.

Only after you win something you will find out its use. Only after you lose something you will find out its value.

Boast neither about your commendation, because it is subjective, nor about someone else's, because it is vainglorious and biased, just wait to hear God's Praise dripping into your soul like dewdrops from rose petals.

Health is fragile like a flower, but paradoxically, does not need to be tended for long. If you use too much water for a flower, you drown it.

Solitude is not isolation. One reflects and lives while meditating about God.

Man's strength comes from Heaven, so does his Divine Soul.

Fortune is a burden on your back. The bigger it gets, the more burdened you are.

Don't ask God for things you yourself can do but ask Him for His blessing in order to accomplish them!

Glorious is the death of someone who knows what they die for!

Any fight is unfair even when we fight for justice. We have to get it in a differently.

When we die, the body is asking the soul to forget it as soon as possible.

The saint who does not have a devil next to him is not real.

Lie smoothers truth, the others mime resuscitation.

An idler, who does not want to work, pretends to be doing something.

The true friendship is not what you express, paradoxically it is just what you avoid, being afraid it might transform itself into something more profound.

The sky is the Earth of our Foreheads.

Ascension is Resurrection from Heaven.

Religion is not a subject to be taught, but a frame of mind to be understood.

Life is like a beam of light, which when it dims, it has lighted its way out.

Only those who sacrifice their Life can bear witness for it.

Love sells wormwood in the spice market.

Visible roots are vulnerable.

By collecting Light in our body, we burn it like martyrs used to.

We share the sins of those people we did not succeed in convincing to repent.

Who lives for himself will have a long life. Who lives for the others will live eternally.

The Moon did not complain it was alone. Consequently, the Stars embraced it.

Just like a mole that sinks its head in the ground, since it has no eyes to see the Sun, atheists strongly oppose to seeing the Light.

When you find excuses for your dreams, you trivialize them.

You cannot miss something you have not lived.

For an unwise man any horizon seems the end of the world.

Don't give me absolution from the guilt of not having done anything!

Come naked to me: I am your coat!

If you really love someone it is not enough to know that person, you must also know what you really are like.

Love is a kind of despair. You cannot continue on your own.

How sad it is to find the explanation of your actions in your guilt!

We live in a cage. The cowards think in a happy mood: "How lucky we are that beasts cannot attack us!"

Our inner fire cannot be put out by a Snow Storm. It can be put out by Carelessness.

The base of our labor is the salt mountain of the sweat that has been dripping down our temples.

Irrespective of how long we may live, it will not be long enough for us to witness the end of time.

Forgiveness should be in accordance with the penitence, not the sin.

Who is afraid of pain, does not have a good communication with his body.

The World Echo is perplexing. The more we talk, the more complicated its sonorities will get.

Any font degenerates into a funeral urn.

Write down your name at the end of a beadroll. God reads them from bottom to top.

Memories make the past seem closer, hopes do the same with the future.

The power of a word lies in its being left unsaid. The most beautiful sermon is when the priest crosses himself.

The loss of life is part of its economy.

The mortal beings who have tasted life, do not want to butter themselves up with the dessert.

Pain should be contagious.

The earth is the narthex of the Sky.

No other victory is greater than the one you have won against yourself.

Don't despair! Time started healing your wounds.

Transfiguration is the Divine Metanoia of each of us, from image to resemblance.

On our way to You there are no wells so we cannot enjoy rest stops.

The wind of despair swells the schooner sails towards God.
Only our soles touch the earth, the rest of our body poise is upwards to God.

Our vertical vector- like body wishes for Heaven as its final destination.

Jesus walked on water in order to save the Apostles' sailing ship from the storm. Miracles happen under our eyes – He did not come under water. We approach a miracle miraculously.

The most evolved beings acutely complain of their imperfection. Man is becoming complete through God.

I have invented my beatitudes. Therefore, they have lasted.

We are a crumble taken from God. Therefore, we shall never crumble

Alas, those who have learnt their lesson! They keep telling it again and again.

Who wants justice should go to Church, not to Law Court.

Happiness is like the Sun: it gives light as long as it is in the Sky.

Christians' persecution has not ceased, but nowadays those who persecute them do not reproach them with Christianity

You are not alone if you have someone in your soul, not next to you.

You have nice dreams only when you sleep in your bed.

God created the World on his own. People appointed consultants in order to diminish their responsibilities and guilt.

The World is like a mirror, when you look at the others you see yourself, too.

The way to Happiness might as well lead you to Disaster. You have to stop at the right time.

A millipede does not dream about snakes.

No one is more powerful than a man who is willing to die.

You are born on the day you start loving, not on the day you were born.

When you pray, God is next to you. When you ask for something, He starts distancing himself from you.

The way to God means climbing, so it is full of impediments. The way to Hell means going down, so it is a continuous and facile fall.

A promise is born when a lie merges with a hope.

It is the consequences of a lie that I am afraid of, not the lie itself.

The most powerful people in the world are those who have lost everything.

When a woman does not cry out at night, she cries out during the day.

Great tragedies are those no one mourns for.

A violin is made from the timber of a tree full of nightingales.

Never give up fighting, remember, your enemy has been given the same advice.

People have the same destiny. Their performances are different.

God creates people first in Heaven.

You do not ask for Liberty, you gain it.

Death does not take farewell from life, but from secular things.

God is in everything, man in what He has left out.

Injustice is amplified by the ignorance of those who accept it.

Who has only eye-witnessed a miracle has already denied half of it.

Happiness is the steam of hot bread and if you share it with several people, it will go higher and higher.

The Russian cosmonauts, when they were up in the Sky, failed to see the angels that Dostoyevsky was able to see from Earth. Humble eyesight amplifies its own acuity.

A cynic asks the doctor to cure him/her only from non-communicable diseases.

Reflection stationed in the brain has no chance in outwitting it.

There are more speculations about the past than there are about the future

That part that dies with us is as old as the soul that goes on living.

We do what we can, and we say we do what we want.

Most people kill us after we die.

The week of Beatitudes starts on Sunday.

I am alone, can you hear the echo…?

There are two people who implore me to live long: the doctor and the banker.

Money is like chaff: it is either blown by wind or it gets useless.

Wealth comes from your soul not your pocket.

What an effort to live, nevertheless no one seems to spare it.

I am much older than my age.

You tell the truth just once because everybody remembers it afterwards.

There comes a time when people do not need you. Then you realize how much you have been appreciated.

We have been banished from Heaven because of vegetarianism.

Since the Genesis people have been making the same mistakes, but they have improved their excuses.

Horses who die on the battlefield believe they will continue grazing after death.

Any time we do not fast, God starves.

The true evils are those that have not happened to us.

Life is not more important than Death. It is more visible.

It is not my fault you don't know me.

I am so famous that I cannot take a leave and walk barefooted in my own house.

Sin is a form of Evil's resistance, an undisturbed form of evil.

We are defined only by what we do every day.

The world has started its Apocalypse. Therefore, anything evil accelerates it.

I have failed my career, I had to choose between being an angel or a man and I have opted for the latter.

People are the Salt of the Earth. They have induced the hypertensive crisis in the World.

The road I have chosen is covered in thorns. It signals the fact I am going in the right direction.

Who reflects on his Happiness kills it.

I have read so much that it prevents me from being original.

The mistakes we are aware of, are sins.

Life is the opportunity of biology to overshoot the mark.

Keep hoping! Something will come true at the end of the day.

I am infinitely lonelier among people than books.

There are more perfect murders than lives.

I am so sad the years keep piling up on me, that I started commemorating my birthdays.

One's physique has nothing to do with one's holiness. If someone is tall it does not mean they are closer to God.

A fallen angel's wings are useless.

The Devil is in a hurry: he knows his time is running short.

Saints are people who have understood their sufferings.

Suffering is in saints' job description.

People die to mess around. Death is a vital desideratum for saints.

I am not afraid of loneliness. Loneliness is afraid of me.

Like all other creatures, people aspire to go to their original habitat –Heaven.

Our world is a kind of Atlantis that commercializes land.

I am the unhappiest angel; therefore, I am not ever going to fall.

God has been expelled from séances because he refused to show up.

All the faults of the world are mine: when a vase is broken somewhere in the Universe my hands are the first to tremble.

When I am alone, I cry out. I do not do it because I want to be heard, I do it to convince myself I am alone.

I have suffered only from communicable diseases. I have not caused any of them.

Happiness, like a bride, is waiting for its Mr. Right.

Who can answer the questions, has asked them themselves before.

Who talks, presumes. Who keeps silence, knows.

The hungry people and the greedy people live on the same Earth.

Don't ask from God to give you proofs of His existence since you have given Him none.

It is sad that both sunset and sunrise happen on the same day!

Each form of relief has a matching disposition in a man's soul.

People die and are born every day.

Life circuit in nature: the sky I see is lower than the sky I feel.

Solitude is unnaturalness of soul and naturalness of spirit.

When you admire a woman, don't start with her dress!

People that are wrong are the first to doubt the other people's fairness.

The people who admire you most are the people who have filled your shoes.

Geniuses make death their future.

Prophets extrapolate. Whatever they wish for themselves comes true for the others.

When you cry out you are heard. When you keep silence, you are understood.

Who is brought handcuffed to the Great Inquest, when they leave they will be free.

Who cries for help when he is alone, has faith.

What is important is not how many we are, but how many we are left.

The fact we all die, does not mean we have to die as we choose.

When mountain climbers reach the peak, they have to decide from where they will start their climbing down, whereas ascetics have to ponder where to build their hermitage.

A lie has to be invented. Truth lies on your lips.

Power is like an edelweiss. The closer you are to the sky, the more difficult it is for somebody to pluck it from you.

Deal with beautiful things! The ugly ones are ready made.

The fact that we are going to die, does not justify the despair we live with.

Christianity is the only form of happy suffering. All the other sufferings are diseases, and the other joy is illusion.

Jesus died sacrificing Himself. He did not die gradually suffering from an illness.

Jesus performed his miracles gradually, so as not to overwhelm us with their brightness.

Beatitudes are all offered in one Sermon, as an integral part that cannot be separated.

A rich man is not happy with his wealth, he is obsessed with it.

Health is a kind of non-communicable disease.

All forms of respect are below mercy

We live remembering. We die hoping.

Patience is cultured indolence.

Multiple talents are co-morbidities, associated illnesses.

Failures are the scars of notable performance.

We live in a cave. The Sun can be brought in only from outside.

We die uncomforted. This is Divine policy.

The mystery of creation cannot be figured out by the creation.

A new mistake is in fact a forgotten mistake.

Life is a suicide which is underestimated by the real suicides.

"I believe you upon your word", does not mean you believe they will do it.

Human Destiny is a priceless fight for Truth.

Ordinary things that happen to us are our forefathers' expectations.

We live in one world, and we die in a different one.

The world's fastest runners go around an Olympic circle.

The wolves that hunt birds suffer from flight nostalgia.

Waiting is time's still-hunting.

Regret is condescendence of pain.

To be an angel you need more than a pair of wings.

Like all strict parents, God wants us perfect.

God is waiting for us in Heaven, while we are improving our comfort on earth.

They do not award prizes for happiness.

People die as they were born, scared of the unknown.

Death takes better care of our soul than life does.

Hope guides us where we want. Despair guides us where it wants.

I am the Atlantan that can invent the Sailing Ship.

Jokes are taken the easy way by those who tell them, and seriously by those who are their victims.

I am an uninspired God: I cannot create a World, but I can pass a judgment on everybody.

We are some field flowers. No matter what colour or scent we have, cattle graze us all the same.

Prizes for the entire career are a kind of aids for funerals.

Young people are convinced they will never grow old. Old people forget they were once young.

Life, as well as Death, wants a quiet place.

Not knowing why you are happy, does not make you feel unhappy.

When the trees are in blossom it does not matter who planted them.

Prudence has transformed vespers into matins.

The most unpopular people are those who always tell the truth.

I bequeath my online manuscripts to everybody.

Surgeons are the only physicians who do not send you to a chemist's.

You are crying upon God in earnest, while you are in an ambulance than when you are in a hearse.

People may be sad, but happiness does not suit them either.

Someone who does not want to get involved personally says "God help you!"

Destiny is the wind that makes the dust fly, while the mountain looks at it impassively.

Dust can rise higher than a mountain peak, but no one appreciates its ascension.

Predator fish in an aquarium dies from depression caused by loneliness.

An experienced godmother sees about the bride's lingerie.

Only the birds which cannot fly, fluff up.

We put in pawn our days for a night of love.

Beggars are extremely efficient. They earn relying on their shortages.

Carelessness is active oblivion.

Chromosomes are blue blooded cousins.

I die like some others live: thinking about the future.

Who wants to tell me something nice, let them write it down!

God has grown old. It is snowing.

We live thinking about death and die thinking about life. This is the Hegelian antagonism of our aspirations.

The Universe is everything evil that can happen in a given space.

Immortality —the desire to live somewhere else.

The softer a pray is the louder it sounds.

"Go away!", I said to the devils. They heard me and drew closer.

Holiness, the Heavenly Glory, has to be deserved here on earth.

'My Lord, do not forgive our trespasses as we forgive those who trespass against us! Forgive them like you and only you can do!'

The sacrifice that does not end with Resurrection is the Apocalypse.

God wants us thirsty, not hungry.

Injustice starts outside us. Justice starts inside us.

My Lord, cleanse my soul with my tears!

Kneecaps, on which we pray, are a Ferris wheel of our impetus to God.

After God created the world, the Devil started criticizing it.

Would you like to be powerful? Decline your power!

We appeal to God instead of calling him.

Even the lion, the king of animals, has to lie in the lurch when hunting.

Work is the oscillation of soul in our body.

People have to work for a week to enjoy a day off.

Don't mock your happiness, take it seriously!
Ivy is a vegetal piece of chalk.

Silence strengthens wisdom, but compromises spontaneity.

A dwarf knows that if the sun shines on him from a suitable angle his shadow can be bigger than that of a giant.

Champions do not need praises. Losers do need them.

The sobriety of some devils compromises angels' good will.

Measles is the evil that comes out of skin. With children it is benign.

Tell me the correct time so I will be able to know how long it is till my life ends.

Sacrifice does not mean doing something for yourself.

Children who have not been punished by their parents are punished by fate. Parents punish tenderly, fate punishes ruthlessly.

God has not planted perfection in man, as He wanted him to aspire for it.

Divorce is about comparing the wife and the mistress.

When God calls your name, your impulse is to open the window, and not the door.

If you want a lesson about the value of money, ask a rich man to lend you some.

God has endowed crows with wings. He did it because He didn't want us to crave for ours.

Death, that is so much blamed, has made several heroes.

As long as the wool is on the sheep, moths do not live in it.

God is everywhere, but the Devil pretends he has sent Him.

Keep asking! They will feel ashamed in the end and will not be able to refuse you.

Alas, the happy man, for he is happy only today.

The girl who is always away, is left on the shelf.

The bald- headed man is always looking for a hat.

If you ignore your enemies, they may believe you have become friends.

Who praises you pretends he/she knows you. Who curses you is convinced he/she knows you.

When the nail and the hammer fight, the result is a beautiful house.

A bee dies on the very day it cannot fetch honey any more.

The fox does not know which hen is hatching, but it finds the very one by chance.

When the sack is threadbare, the flour is spread on the floor.

Even helped by the stars, the Moon does not emit as much light as the sun.

A woman is like wine, after she makes you tell the truth, she fools you into believing she will keep it.

I am a saint, only God knows for how long.

Who wants to write, can find paper and pencil.

If the emperor does not have a crown, his guardsmen do not have weapons.

The pig would run away, but where else will it find another slop basin full of food?

A kind man does not have to be called out. He knows when he is needed.

Don't tell the saints what God already knows.

Without dregs, the juice of grapes does not get sour, but it does not turn into wine either.

Go where you want but come back in time! Go where you are supposed to go but come back when you want!

A jar of honey without a lid does not get sour, but it attracts flies.

A handsome man looks for a beautiful woman, whereas a wise guy looks for a wise woman.

A good horse takes its master home, and not into the battle.

Put yourself out of a fool's way, because he/she wants to know how much room there is for him/her!

The fool laughs at the farmers who come from work every day, but load and carry the harvest only once a year.

He doubts everything but lies.

He wants a wedding, but he already has several wives.

He hired some musicians, but he is still looking for a wife.

The merry man of the village is not the sage but the fool.

He is sticking his tongue out hoping the doctor will believe him.

I am fed up with what has happened to me, whereas God is fed up with what He has created.

I am hungry, not because I have not eaten, but because of what I have seen.

In the poor man's bowl, the food does not get sour.

You miss what you like, even when they are near you.

When the devil is on his way, the trouble has already arrived.

The priest has a barrel of holy water, but he does not give all of it away.

It is the mane not the roar that makes the lion King.

An ant stressed because of hard work becomes a termite.

The devil would not be powerful if he had not called to his support a couple of angels.

The wind that helps you with the seeding, hinders your harvesting.

My darling, I am coming back to you like God to the World: the more imperfect you are the more interested in you I am.

The black holes are the heavenly places that used to belong to the fallen angels.

Heaven's Light can be seen under a priest's stole when someone confesses their sins.

A smiling mouth is no longer hungry.

At Resurrection time those who will not be able to give up on their sumptuous burial vaults will be dead.

Don't come back out because you will run into yourself!

A lie together with a cohort of servants cannot depose the unguarded Truth.

When both the Sun and the Moon are in the sky, one cannot see well.

Courage looking for peril is insane.

God asks you how you are, and you tell Him about your illnesses.

I do not miss you. I miss what we used to do together.

I woman cooks for you if you have hugged her.

He is standing in the way like a poplar, casting no shade and bearing no fruit.

Boast with your actions not with your power!

He is not sure of himself, but he is sure of me.

Beautiful people blossom, good people bear fruit.

Who says they cannot run, have not seen the wolf.

Sugar is sweet but should not be in a soup.

Someone who is going to hang themselves but does not want to die, chooses the lowest branch

It is the Priest not the bell that often persuades you to come to church.

If a donkey had a whistler, it would consider itself a shepherd.

Bad illiterate people are animals, whereas bad literate people are devils.

While you are waiting, you are wasting your lifetime.

Night darkens the Earth but cannot cast a shade.

Who asks the Devil to judge them, will be punished by God.

If you give the grape juice to your children, you will not get drunk the rest of the year.

Brave people get well without a doctor and die without a priest.

Burning love soon dies out.

A man takes off a woman's clothes, but she puts them back on.

If all nanny-goats had scabies, Billy-goats would not hold their horns up.

If you don't catch the hare, the wolf will.

A ewe does not have horns, but no ram can settle it harsh.

It is better to be humble in God's name than rich and helped by the devil.

The law you are afraid of, has been passed for people like you.

You have your grains ground at the mill, but you take home the flour already ground. When it comes to culture you take your forefathers' harvest and use it to make your descendants grow.

Your contemporaries praise you, posterity appreciates you.

The rich fast, the poor starve.

When the boar sees the sow, it forgets to ask it how the previous years' piglets are.

You don't die from death you die from oblivion.

Even when the devil has an angel tiara, it wears it over its horns.

In the dressmaker's opinion all your clothes are old-fashioned.

Don't give steak to a thirsty man or water to a hungry man!

A man is happier for something he has not experienced. God loves you and a priest says this is his merit.

He attended the vigil as he wanted to meet the dead man.

Don't punish yourself! There are many others who can do a better job!

Don't take your wife with you when you go to a fair, people may believe she is for sale!

Your wife loves you before she gives birth to your first child.

The longing in me comes from thee.

It is not the thieves I am afraid of, but the hinges, because they are rusted.

If you don't like to stay in, don't get yourself a bride!

The lamb looks for the ewe and the ewe looks for the ram.

He came back poor, and on top of all he got married.

Cuckoo bird sings but it does not hatch the eggs.

People die every day, but one can hear bells toll only on holidays.

Don't brag although I do not know you!

A horse runs only before it comes across alfalfa.
Gold is the same, only its price varies from day to day.

Respect your enemies! Only your parents should be treated like icons.

Mud seems to be gold in the sunshine.

Girls blush both when you kiss them and when you tell them they allowed you to kiss them.

A barren tree is not shaken, but it ends up in a stove.

I have no time to waste. All I want is to have a rest.

A woodpecker pecks only hollow tree.

He would move the mountains but unfortunately his back aches

The Devil teaches us everything we were taught at school, but it is his lessons we remember.

When a horse chases a mare, the coachman does not need to drive it.

It is raining, but not on the poor man's farming land.

He is wearing his Sunday best although it is Monday morning.

Truth without justice is like the Sun in a different Sky.

Ignorant people say you have not asked them questions about stuff they know.

When someone breaks a bottle, the party is not over.

Wine makes your blood flow faster but not everywhere in your body.

The club you keep near your bed, can protect you against thieves but only if you are not sleeping.

Good wine delights you, bad wine gets you drunk.

The hen would fly but only as far as the nest.

A lawyer has nothing to teach an honest man.

When a donkey brays all the nightingales take their flight.

Frogs believe fishermen come attracted by their croak, not by the silence of the fish.

If the Sun didn't exist, we could see the Moon during the day, too.

When it is raining the thirsty man cups his hands.

On emptying a barrel, a drunkard would swop it for a jug of wine.

Hail is also rain, but it ruins the crops.

In a Church everybody crosses oneself, whereas the Devil bows down.

Who wants to earn a living, is not at home at lunch time.

You dream about what you do not have, and a nightmare gives you plenty of it.

The hard-working man digs. The lucky man strikes water.

He likes Swiss cheese, but its holes are rather big.

He is drunk, but he would not stay in.

No matter where the Sun is, the front horizon seems brighter.

He can speak all the languages under the sun, but nobody understands him.

He went hunting and caught two fish.

You eat what you have not cooked. You also do what you have not thought.

If you do not call me, I come. If you call me, I run.

We feel sorry for ourselves for everybody else feels sorry for themselves.

The devil never stands in the way of a man who is running.

Flying birds do not need the grains given in a back yard.

One is never alone if they have a mirror or a book.

As long as you do not know what the other life is like, don't give up on the life you know about!

Hope is the greatest delusion. You make a promise to yourself.

A non -believer believes in photos, not in icons.

Let his glass be full, for he will drink to the health of strangers!

A spiffed-up man does not have time for other qualities.

When he is asking from you, he also has a sack ready in his pocket.

The seeds make the pumpkin blow up.

Some people clean using a sweep, some other their wit.

An upstart who used to be a servant, cannot help begging.

When the Moon is up, the wife is out in the neighbourhood.

Who has siblings, does not need friends.

Don's shear the sheep when the icy north wind is blowing! Put on the coat made of the last year's wool!

Don't show happiness on your face, for it will soon fade away!

When he left, he was on horseback, he came back on foot, but he says he has got rich.

All things made for you by someone else are good.

Who tricks you is your master, and you may not realize it.

He is running home like hell because laziness caught him in the field.

He has plenty of food because all his siblings are employed.

He would be working, but unfortunately it is Sunday.

He is asking for justice, but his dagger is smeared with blood.

It is the distance not the dust that worries the horse.

Who patronizes you, does not want to teach you how to fly.

He would eat, but there is no one there to fetch him a spoon.

He wants to be generous, but he still hasn't chosen the first person to be assisted.

An old master looks for a young apprentice.
He promises not because he intends to keep his word, he does it only to be believed.

As long as we have wine in our barrel, he will visit us. When the wine runs dry, he will get upset.

The crow eats what it finds in the field, the swallow eats what it finds on the porch.

A beautiful bride has a pretentious mother-in-law.

Walk around the world if you want to learn something new!

When they saw his house burning, they fetched some brushwood.

During the vigil a widow does her best to arrange her head kerchief in such a way that it does not cover her face.

There are more deaths among people who are rolling in cash than among those who are hard up.

The Devil comes uninvited and says he hears better than God.

He would not lie to you if you stopped asking him questions.

Any road leads to Rome on condition you end your journey there.

In his dream he saw a horse, but he did not have a halter.

Call me to pay you a visit because I am at your door.

The child you love expects to be your heir.

Don't poke the fire or else everything will burn to the ground.

He would not be eating it if he did not like it.

You still poison yourself even if you eat using your own spoon.

Nights have turned into days for those whose days are numbered.

Love and death want you to lie down.

The lazy man cuts the rooster that is crowing in the afternoon

He marries her to be his lawful wedded wife and, she marries him to be her lawful wedded sugar-daddy.

A loafer pretends he works in winter as well, as he does not want to be the talk of the town.

The hungrier a wolf is, the stronger it gets.

When you give something away, they ask you for the basket as well.

The cock hops aboard to mate with a hen, but at the same time it pecks it at its head.

Dogs are more afraid of a big wolf than the sheep are, but the shepherd is the most frightened of all.

People kiss the miller only when the latter has his cheeks powdered with flour.

Let God take me, but let he take me where I want.

The devil bunches up, God makes room.

His sheep have died, only his donkey is alive.

His Luck has left, but his troubles are still with him.

The poplar has a lot of leaves, but all of them tremble.

There are great people even in small villages.

A wolf whose stomach is full when it goes past a sheepfold it fears even a donkey's shadow.

He has taken a day off because he has a job to do.

The loafer makes money like a bumblebee honey.

He would like to die, but he does not have the heart to give away.

When you are talking about love you should be half naked.

You can lie to me, but you cannot make me believe you.

When it is snowing all the sheep are white and the donkey is wearing a mantle.

If there were no illnesses, people would kill each other.

He has pricked on a nail and now he claims it is his.

He has patience but he does not know what to do with it.

He has locked himself in and now he does not know where the exit is.

The chain falls if only one single link breaks.

When you see a wolf, run for your life even among the nettles!

When you have no other choice, does not mean you have patience.

When body eats, the soul grasps for air.

The blind man says he cannot see, but when he is holding some money, he knows how to count it.

With every wave a jellyfish gets closer to the shore, but it never gets on it.

Who longs for somebody, waits for them on the porch.

When you bake bread for him, he wants some sponge cake.

He says he is so hungry that he would eat anything, but he is asking what she has for dessert.

The grape vine of a heavy drinker produces less than a litre of grape juice.

The Sun smiles even at the clouds that cover it.

The donkey says its ears prevent it from catching up with the stallion. What if it were shod...

The more money a drunkard has, the sooner he dies.

He wants to be alone, but to enjoy it, he summons a council.

He was not eaten by the wolf in the forest, but he was slapped by his wife for being late.

A wolf lurks where grass is lush.
He went out for wild strawberries and came back with nettles.

Homeland is only yours. The world is yours as well.

God receives people's words with the help of saints, while prayers reach Him by themselves.

Shepherds forget to milk the stray sheep.

Jesus was seen even by sinners. God was not seen by anybody, not even by saints.

He would have shot himself, but he had only a knife.

He wants to run away, but there was no wolf to frighten him.

When a priest gets hungry, he grants dispensation from fasting.

A proud pig does not agree to be scratched.

He is victorious only by using the back door.

He has not seen his friend since he lent him some money.

We can say to each other "I love you" sincerely only when we are animated by love.

God created the world out of love, not out of nothing.

A knight kneels down on one knee only, while the believer kneels down on both;

Love is a venereal disease. Both partners catch it.

A monkey can hold a pen with its legs, but it cannot write poetry.

The world has never belonged to men, but women have known since the very beginning how to make them believe it does.

You run more slowly when you are wearing the champion medal round your neck.

Women are gold mines. Their passion for jewels is redundant.

Time mocks at beautiful women and glorifies the ugly ones.

The longer women's legs are the more inaccessible they are.

Destiny waits for you, just to show you have failed.
Vanity is pride caressed on its head.

Women are like Snow White. They need the seven dwarves to help them to meet the Prince.

Breasts are women's elbows- they jostle with them to make room.

When you lie down in your matrimonial bed you are not tired and when you wake up, you are exhausted.

Women who can undress quickly have studied the movements.

Children who are not born out of love do not meet their parents, so they cannot reproach them for it.

A woman has legs to walk up to her beloved man and run away from all the other men.

If you stop paying compliments to your wife, she may suspect you. If you pay her too many compliments, she may still suspect you.

A woman that scolds her lover is divorced.

When the wife and the mistress are one, keep them company in turn!

God took a day off after He created the woman.

Statistics say there are more women than men. Those few extra women left unloved, play havoc in the world.

I am in love with a woman, but I forgot which one.

The women who are not wearing high heeled shoes, have taken them off.

Men with principles do not take mistresses.

Ulysses cheated on Penelope only with women who couldn't weave.

When a woman wants to go to the theatre and a man wants to make love, a total bedlam breaks out there.

Men conquered the world first and then they let themselves conquered by women.

The tragedy in a marriage is that man comes across the same woman both in the bedroom and the kitchen.

When a beautiful woman appears both men and women turn their heads, but in different directions.

Women hope their beauty will last till the day their husbands become impotent.

A woman who wants the moon in the sky does not have what she needs by her.

Don't take in your arms a woman who is running desperately to you! For sure her husband is coming after her.

A woman who demands that she should be told the truth would rather like her suppositions to be confirmed.

The good thing about marriage is that, no matter how long it last, sooner or later, comes to an end.

Women put on nice clothes because they want men to admire them, but for what they are like not for their smart outfits.

Don't run away from a woman! She always runs faster than you.

Whenever one speaks about women, their mothers are exceptions to the rules.

Women lied only to those who asked them questions.

Voyeurism started when a man was first asked by a woman: "Do you like me?"

No sooner had God made the woman than Saint Peter opened the Heaven's Gate.

The riskiest loves are those in the Paradise, because they happen under the very eyes of God.

A marriage proposal is full of mistakes. A divorce sentence is absolutely flawless.

Who can forgive a womanizer? All married men.

Cleopatra was so beautiful that the Roman Empire tried to conquer her every day.

The real sacrifice is to sacrifice oneself for someone who does not deserve it.

A superior man can see with his ears and hear with his eyes.

Death is a crawler that needs a lifetime to get to us.

As long as we are alive, we are permanently uncertain.

If there is no one you can ask for permission, does not mean that whatever you do, is legal.

If you can say why you love someone, then you do not love.

I move throughout my life in all directions like a sparrow.

Doctors' and priests' credibility are affected by their mortality.

Daily living is indeed a big responsibility.

I would have learnt a lot if, from time to time, we had died for a while.

If you have a car, you have an advantage. You don't go to work on foot, you are tugged.

All people are volunteers, but each of them volunteers for something else.

God always understands us, the Devil only when we make mistakes.

Money is the main means of respect among people.

A man's power is the power of all the people who have stood up against him.

Both a happy and an unhappy day is twenty- four hours long.

Who is waiting for his happiness down on his knees, will receive it lying down.

God created the Earth for all the people. God created the Sky for only One.

With eastern people faith is greater than will. With western people it is quite the other way around.

People are like flowers. If you take the earth away from them, they will stop blossoming.

Since they removed Adam's rib it has been stinging him harder.

Cows may graze as much grass as they want, they can produce milk, but they can't calve without a bull.

A woman's great charm is the fact that she truly loves her man although in the beginning she considers him a hero and then a child.

The fount of tears is in the soul, not in the eyes.

A man's eyes fill with tears when a woman chops onion next to him or when he remembers that woman.
I am younger than my age.

Like Jesus, we were born to be killed, not to die.

As our souls are in putrefaction, perfume industry became necessary.

Without a biro a writer is lost.

I am dead drunk. This is the only state under which I accept death.

I am a net full of fish. Saint Peter left me in the sea water and went away with Jesus.

We are romantic, especially when we are not making love.

For us it is impossible to see God. He is beyond the Sun.

Writers die with a ball point pen in their hands just like the Romanian medieval rulers who used to die with a sword in their hands.

A conflict of ideas is a civil war between cerebral circumvolutions.

When hymen breaks, the spell is broken.

I am sipping the coffee grounds. I am interiorizing my Destiny.

No poet harvests quinces in order to eat them.

No matter how magnanimous a snail might be, it cannot accommodate a slug in its shell.

If people, like flowers, were pollinated by bees, those in love would be walking about with swarms of bees flying after them

I am a social hermit.

I am a serial, whose plot takes everybody by surprise, myself included.

Steps lead me anywhere they want. Hands are under my control.

A complex truth is packed with lies.

Women in love look in men's eyes, those who out of love, look in the purse mirror.

If Achilles had had only one leg, he would not have died.

Truth stays hot even after it gets cold. Sip it slowly!

I am intoxicated just like a plum in a bottle of alcohol. Nobody can drink me, but I give my flavour to them.

We cry both when we are born and when we die. I have never understood why they say we do it for joy the first time, and for sorrow, the second time.

Don't think about death while you are alive! You will have all the time in the world to do it afterwards.

Life always sieges Death and the latter gives in, only when it will.

Poverty jumps off the back of a man who goes to work.

I am tone-deaf. I applaud both Beethoven and Brahms.

If a swan did not sing when it dies, it would be just an exquisite goose.

That part by Bach that is not repetitive is just monotonous.

The Moon lights the whole night, but the fireflies ignore it.

Life and Death are contagious, but one of them can catch Death without touching it.

If the frogs did not croak, one would hear the fish.

Artists have created Renaissance while Christians have created Resurrection.

When I realize that, in spite of the fact that I keep running I get nowhere, I started running the marathon.

When a beautiful woman is speaking, you feel like kissing her, if she is also wise, you feel like listening to her.

Just like the large mountain ranges formed by folding, so did my forehead wrinkles.

When I had my first book edited, the Nobel Prize for literature was not awarded.

Romania has enough destiny for two not just one history.

Wheat grows the same way rain falls, vertically.

Our inside world is larger than our outside world. Paradoxically the soul fits our body.

The world seen by the blind exceeds the sight through pupils.

No matter how much a dog loves its master, it cannot help fawning on the butcher.

A man is born in labour pains; therefore, pain is his first knowledge of the world. Any future pain will increase his knowledge.

Jesus meets His Father when He is on the cross.

While alive we are getting farther and farther from God, but when we die, we are getting closer.

The whole Earth is surrounded by a kind of air-earth atmosphere.

If God is everywhere in the world, then there is no room left for the Devil.

I pray to God, to avoid praying to a man.

I am being waited for, like a freight train in a marshalling yard.

Although worms are uglier, they are less dangerous than viruses.

It takes dying not living to be born.

Grown-ups are children who go to Academies instead of going to kindergartens.

Man is a symbol, which is taken literally by his fellow people and figuratively only by God.

People die in order to be appreciated.

Life is an extended vigil.

Explanations only complicate guilt.

Death has all the ingredients of life: honours, fights and revenges.

Death has eternity on its side but unlike life it has plenty of time.

Death is a gift you get when you are born. Avoid unpacking it as long as you can.

Common sense teaches us that when we fight, we should whisper.

Joy is secular happiness.

When you are baptized, they sprinkle you with holy water, when you die with holy tears.

Martyrdom is the continuation of life.

Soldiers go to war with the thought of coming back alive not victorious.

For biologists a butterfly is only a winged caterpillar.

We are like a spring that flows only downhill. Our flow increases while we are getting towards the river mouth.

When a dictator dies, people give away for their dear departed relatives.

Life is a drunken state and death the hangover after. The better the wine is, the sweeter the hangover.

Life is like a bracket. It is important what comes after it.

Only that part of the body that has not been dipped into the holly water dies, which is everything that is heavier than a baby.

People hope that when they die, they will find two easy-to-read placards "Heaven" and "Hell". They are wrong. There is only one, reading "Don't jump over the fence!"

Help yourselves to the daintiest dishes on the table of Life. After this feast you will have to travel for a long time.

Everything happens at the right time, the trouble is we are all in a hurry, like some watches wanting their second hands.

A very ambitious man is like a fruit tree that seems to be in blossom, but in fact it is smothered by the white veil woven by caterpillars.

When Death calls the roll, those who have been called do not have time to say "Here".

No one trusts the After Life. The evidence is that everybody lives this life to the full.

People would spend a fortune to live, but they prefer doing it for free, praying.

Sins make our life more beautiful, but shorter, too.

I fear God, and the devil terrifies me.

Moliere died on stage. How many actors dared to play his part afterwards?

Only the bed of young couples' squeaks

Although there are so many people in a cemetery, we feel lonely.

No matter how much God loves us, the keys are with Saint Peter.

Mourners, go after the hearse while enemies are waiting at the tomb.

Good news does not need a megaphone.

We all die, a few of us live.

I go jogging in my spare time. I run to work.

We mock Life, and Death mocks us.

I am the most reliable narrator of my life.

How little we believe in the After Life! None of us packs any spare clothes.

If stupid people admitted their stupidity, smart people would not give up on their position.

Death is a cat. Man is a mouse. The more difficult it is for death to catch it, the longer it teases it.

Whatever you have learnt in your life, you implement in the Afterlife.

Man fiddles about and Death puts him on the shelf for a while.

How long does Death last? It depends on one's religion.

Life does not know what to begin with. Death has patience.

Death does not understand why dying people always call for a doctor, since it is permanently available.

It would be a pity not to use a tomb in which you have invested.

If we could choose our death, we would choose a forgetful one

My death has grown up together with me.

Death carries out its mission every day, wars make it feel tired.

Death does not wear high heels. It says it could not walk that much. On top of all, it would make a lot of noise…

During the holidays Death looks after the holidaymakers.

Death is on Earth. Life is in the After Life.

Death has only one demand. He won't be blamed for killing the drunkards and the smokers.

Death knows that, for some suicides, no one will dedicate temples to him.

Life is Death in disguise, but we realize it, only at the last moment, when it takes off its mask.

Life is a Supper, but without Jesus we are having it in a refectory.

We all are under house arrest. We cannot exchange it when we wish.

A swan always sings for a reason.

Any moment both Life and Death claim the same man.

When we are alive, we are sentenced to live.

Silence is the most profound answer, it includes everything.

A man does not live as long as he wants to, but as he wants to.

If the Sun weren't brave to appear when the rain was in full swing, there would be no rainbow.

My life did not begin on my birthday, but on a night of passionate love, nine months before.

Take days off only at the weekend, otherwise the boss will notice.

It is difficult to die like a lion after leading a dog life.

Life is about everything that can happen to you on earth, on condition you are not a pilot.

Life has no right to ask anything from you, unlike you, who can ask everything from it.

Man gets everything he needs from life, but he realizes it, only when he dies.

Love of God is love for your neighbour. That is why very few get to it.

Death makes life unrepeatable.

If there is no one you can smile at, smile at yourself in the mirror.

You can climb up to the sky without a ladder, but you certainly need one to climb down.

I am the most inspired when I am sleeping. I have some fantastic dreams.

Man believed he was free when his chain got long enough.

God must have an answering machine in order to listen to so many prayers.

After death, ghosts have nothing to do with bodies, but souls do.

Now and then people raise against those they have elected.

Life is an air mattress onto which we, the hedgehogs, venture to jump.

Fanciful people are either artists or scholars. The difference between them is the fact that artists have not found a practical side of their fantasy, yet.

The piece of bad news is always a different one.

David taught us that we can fight with stones against monstrous creatures.

By using the Trojan Horse, Ulysses did not win, he just put an end to a ten- year- long siege.

Happiness seizes you like a bench vice and you can no longer move.

The most expensive book could be a mobile telephone directory.

I have never written for rich people. If I had had, my books would have been more expensive.

At the end of the Genesis God ran out of materials and resorted to men to make the woman. The advantage is that the two are so much alike that they sometimes get on well.

The hinds sip fertile rivers of mating out of the dew gathered in its hooves.

Romanticism volatilizes art that was already diaphanous.

We are some mountains washed by the sea. We are taller than we seem.

I run for my life every day.

Death has something against me. It keeps avoiding me.

God does not give us what we want too soon. He knows that beggars at the Church door go home as soon as they are given something.

A horse with a thorn in its leg can win the race.

I am the prisoner of my own states of mind.

The author is in his work like a worm in an apple. If he/she remains there for too long, he/ she destroys it.

What wonderful books could come out, if the newspapers were archived!

I have made up my mind. I will get old when I am ninety something years old.

Mephisto would have been a kind devil if he had not bought Faust's soul.

There is an explanation for everything that happens in this world, which makes everything terrifying.

I am ready to sell my soul for next to nothing. Faust has messed the market.

If you sell someone else's soul, you are a Judah i.e., a criminal, if you are Faust, you are a genius.

I can't help wondering where people still find resources to die.

God has banished us from Heaven to make us strive for it.

The road to Heaven cannot ignore Golgotha.

I keep looking after myself day in, day out. No wonder I am getting limited.

I am a slave of my timid freedom.

I do not know how to write prose. Every sixth word rhymes.

The foreplay begins when you start rolling your hair, waiting for me.

A man is what his fellow people allow him to be.

Polygamy has been replaced with mistresses.

Believers tell the truth, philosophers give an explanation to it and scientists harness it to produce electricity.

Pure wool with no synthetic fibers is eaten by moths.

Nails outlive us since they continue growing. They are like lies which are not annihilated as soon as the truth is told.

I can see the world better with my fingertips than with my eye -slots.

Scheherazade is the only woman who saved her life by telling stories, and not by making love.

The beggar who jingles his small money-since he does not have money to buy himself a violin-is thought to be rich and no one gives him a penny.

I am so complicated that I am asking myself whether I am the pinnacle of mankind.

I have been dead for years. My advantage is that I have already eaten all my memorial meals.

I am a contortionist –my soul is eight-shaped. Now I am doing my best to unknot it.

Human species is like a football match. It scored and preserved the result. It neither takes advantage nor progress, it just preserves itself for fear it might lose everything.

I am looking at the sky through a telescope. At the other end is God's eye that sees me small, tiny, itsy-bitsy.
We walk on water not like Jesus, but like water fleas.

I am pedantic. It is not about my frame of mind. It is about the fact it takes me an hour to dress.

Some people frame their diplomas. Unlike them, I frame my childhood photos.

I am my life's Black Tuesday.

My drama is that I do not live in the world I imagine.

I have a problem with my eyes. I can see beyond the horizon line.

If I had been Shakespeare's contemporary, I would not have missed any of his premieres. How snobbish of me!

All the women I undressed, bore a grudge against me.

A man cannot wait to make love, and a woman is looking forward to giving him an opportunity.

Chronos is crazy after Vivaldi's "Seasons".

Doomsday does not frighten me, but the end of my life does.

I had some exceptional teachers. Each of them told me I had no talent for their subject.

Life has no sequels. Death is a continuation.

A wife, who is asking you where the blonde hair on your shirt collar is from, gives herself away.

People who are in love are fond of numerology.

There are two things that come to an end too soon: a sex party and this wretched life.

Saints are superior to angels, because they do not need wings to ascend.

I landed on the moon together with Neil Armstrong. I am still there.

My porch has thousands of flowers and no woman.

I am living inside me. If I do not move out in a year, I will have it renovated.

I am feeling lonely. Finally, I am alone.

Jelly fish in shallow water are as frightened as whales are in deep water.

If the Snake got to the moon, it could get there only crawling to it.

Healing potions in big dozes can kill you.

A forbidden love is waiting for at every turn. All we have to do is to refuse to turn our head.

If people were really merciful, there would be neither Law Courts nor Banks.

I doubt myself the same as I doubt the Big Fat Liar.

I am an unshod horse but by running I have become hoofless.

I have been messing about in my life as if I were on a platform in a country station, where nobody knows why trains are late.

If we succeed in being able to understand each other, it means that we are geniuses.

When a turkey is fan-tailed, it does not see the grains it is fed with.

We are wonderful any time we succeed in being who we really are.

When a woman turns her head in surprise looking at you, it means you have grown old.

It is great to marry young, but it is not so good if it lasts for ever.

I am travelling through life like a tram on its route. I do it nonstop both ways.
I am not a man. I am his quest.

I am motivated only by what I have not done. I feed on vacuum.

A robot is not more than a man, but together they are more than two people.

Music does not have enemies. There are enough instrumentalists.

Angels have their own wrinkles that appear where they fold their wings.

I have had a strange dream. I had a dream about where I was sleeping.

I am being introduced to my own thoughts and I insist on them calling me on my first name.

We have in common everything that separates us.

Love is the only form of liberty soul asks for.

The Nobel Prize for Peace is awarded even during the wars.

Mother is the first woman our eyes catch sight of, and the last one our eyes will embrace.

Paradoxically, the same mother who pushes us out into this world, during birth labours, as if she wanted to get rid of us, cuddles us immediately after.

A masochist is happy when he suffers. A Christian is happy that when he suffers nobody else does.

Past is such a changeable time, due to our memory tricks. It is more fascinating and richer than future which is just one.

On the chess board, both a pawn and the king can be moved the same way.

Work teaches you three bad things: to be happy doing it for eight hours every day, to feel well, although you are sweated and to celebrate a day off by work.

I am my own slave: I have been working myself all day long.

I want to breathe oxygen. I am not interested in carbon dioxide.

The fool who has not learnt how to lie is doomed to failure.

I dream big for others, never for me.

When I have finished with principles, I will start with ideas.

I have a headache because of everything that happens to me. My rheumatism is at my forehead bone.

The richer the deceased is, the more serious the people who attend the vigil are.

"Yes and no" is the answer nobody can use to contradict you.

Monks are saints in mourning, some half-mast-ed angels.

My desire to leave is part of Brownian movement.

I want nothing from God now. I can get closer to Him at last.

Believers have finally learnt the lesson and do not ask God for food when they are fasting.

The problem with the Romanians is that they have always been given orders in a foreign language.

The most dangerous devil is the one who works hard.

My Lord, some people behave as if they knew your telephone number.

The insincere people should be asked questions beating about the bush.

Oedipus knew that the answer was in the riddle of the Sphinx.

Most people answer the questions that we do not feel like asking.

An answer is the lightning rod of a question.

Monocle is the equivalent of glasses worn by the erudite Cyclops.

Cyclops, who could see everything when asked to cover one eye, failed the sight test.

A mole has no eyes, but it feels with its snout when there is light.

Most people should be under letter "A" in a telephone directory – "A" from anonyms.

I do not despair I am anonymous as long as God Himself is the greatest anonym.

I sometimes compete with a dreamer, but nightmares are my disadvantages.

They put photos of the departed ones on the cross, photos taken when they were young, to clarify the moment when their life was disrupted.

What I want from God, He wants from me as well. How can we harmonize?

I am carrying my soul in my chest pocket.

A boxer who knocks the opponent out, is in fact, a woman in disguise.

If you are happy, you are vulnerable, as you do not care whether somebody else can take it away from you.

Happiness is a trance-like state: you are half dead.

God can grant us anything. That is the rub, we should not ask Him for just anything.

If we are afraid of Devil, we hurt God.

God is by us, no matter where we may run.

Without God we may lose our human status as well.

When I arrived at a "simple past", she had already left for a "past perfect."

A life measured in years, compromises its living.

Life is more than someone has lived.

The hare that gets a paw caught in a trap turns into an advocate.

Most people lose their mind without psychiatrists' consent.

The prudent driver leaves his cat at home.

What Caligula did, was to speak in Latin everywhere in Olympus.

I am reconciling with the devil, so that God should not be angry with me.

During the Religious Education classes pupils learn, first of all, to stop cheating.

God gives a passing mark to those who have flunked RE.

A poor man says: "I have bought a raincoat that also protects me from the sun."

Judah would have kissed even the apostles, but they had run away.

On Sunday, during the liturgy, believers are given flight lessons.

The butterfly has a lot of energy in flight because the caterpillar has eaten enough leaves.

We are happy if we do our best not to panic.

The whole world is a chaos. Take it from me as I have had an important contribution.

I am a Ninja warrior. I don't have a sword, but I can yell like one.

In a clay mug the unfermented wine juice must taste the same as in a grape.

Even a toothless guy looks better when he smiles.

I am begging the farmers to sow wheat on my grave. I don't think I deserve so much ground.

The toothless snake envies the legs of a lizard.

Some eagles soar above the peaks only to pinpoint the corpse upon which they will rush.

Nobody wants to leave the earth without first taking counsel with a doctor, then with a notary and finally with a priest.

I can tell you the truth, but I cannot explain it to you.

Who is more than fifteen minutes late, has got on a wrong train.

If they don't give me the change, I consider it a tip.

Sociologists' associations do not consist of people but of living entities.

I am an altruist. I am willing to divorce for my wife's sake.

The mouse: "I was lucky, the black cat that crossed my path didn't see me."

Everybody, except the takers, is allowed to bunch up.

What is killing me about my destiny is that I have to wait.

With God and angels, I talk the same. I do not want to upset them by treating Him preferentially.

A hungry lion is no longer the king of the jungle.

I hope at the Last Judgment, we will be called one by one.

Any plank in the fence is a possible pole that the neighbours could have used to fight with if they themselves had not built the fence.

How happy you feel when you lose an empty wallet!

Heaven is a kind of Los Angeles, its lights can be seen from a distance.

With women, shading tears and menstrual period have a similar mechanism, they happen periodically.

I am striving to tell you the truth and you are striving not to understand it.

The defeat of time is history's only success.

God has made the earth round as He wanted the world to be perfect.

Infinite is as far as and beyond God.

Caesar was stabbed with twenty- three knives on the Ides of March. Only one of them hurt him, his adopted son's.

Woman's masculinity is stronger than man's femininity.

God promises and Saints keep the promise.

If you want to be an angel, God has to acknowledge it.

Human species is in danger of extinction. How else can they explain the fact they mourn so much each and every departure?

The jester in me has retired. I still have two unused paint tubes left.

The pact with the devil is always unilateral.

The more blossoms a fruit tree has in spring the more fruit it will bear in autumn.

I am a long-haired guy, wooing Delilah.

God is waiting for us. Jesus is welcoming us.

I think, therefore, I am fiddling about with myself.

The Sunday clothes and the burial clothes are on the coat hangers close to each other.

The ability of the hunter to shoot accurately drives the deer crazy.

Only by resigning can I get rid of the long expectancy, whose addict I am.

I have broken the record of walking on a wire. The wire was spread on the ground.

I can sip the morning bitter coffee till noon.

Soul, the hard core of the body, is nevertheless, perishable.

How carelessly we throw away the placenta, after we are born! This carelessness, towards what fed and protected us, will haunt us throughout our life.

What ill-sorted association! Chess, the most rational game, shares the same box with backgammon, the euphoria of hazard.

How many of the wedding guests will attend the funeral years later?

The woman's milk has been coveted by all the lovers, but she gives it only to her baby.

Some people live their life on tiptoe, like an ermine that is afraid to smear itself.

Mythology is Astrology with humans.

Cornucopia can no longer be used as a musical instrument.

I am the postman of God. I have not found anyone at home so far.

Opinion Polls are statistical opinions.

I rely on God, but this relation is not reciprocated.

Neither a bear nor a man dies every time they whine.

Success is not supposed to come up with justifications.

Meticulous people are meticulous even when they make a mistake.

I dislike a podium. I suffer from vertigo.

When they tell the truth, many people rely on their audience's credulity.

Life is a permanent back and fore between Heaven and Hell.

I am a hermeneut of the Baroque and I have an interrogative pattern.

A man who cries cannot be bad.

We must love each other and not fight to the bitter end. Statistically speaking, of all those who oppose, only half of them are right.

I want to be weak, for those who are weak are caressed.

Mercy is the first form of getting to know God.

Judging by how fast I grow up, I should change my ID card every day.

Heart is the channel in time's water.

Life means having the patience of constantly breathing.

The world belongs to God, but people fight for it.

Through dream, during the night, God keeps the light in us on.

It is snowing. God is paying attention to us.

When we don't understand something, we are sad. It is obvious we are born to learn.

The only difference between poker and chess is the stake.

Romanians and nature are siblings, like Cain and Abel.

The revolution of the Sun in the sky is predictable. This does not make it less solemn.

The theatre of the absurd was not created before Samuel Becket and Eugene Ionesco since life was not absurd before.

Your enemies are your ex-friends to whom you have nothing else to offer.

Initially the ants under an elephant's sole used to be happy because they were shaded.

In the After Life, it is a shame to repeat the same mistakes.

I am not like Odysseus' sailors. I feel attracted more by the mermaids' breasts and less by their songs.

I like tasting the honey of life spread over the salt of death.

No genuine artist can create longer than a week. God is an example.

Art is cultivated prostitution- beauty in exchange for money.

I am feeding the ravens of my not-yet-interred body.

I am moving backwards like a crab, but the sea is not in that direction.

I suffer from sorrow like camels from dropsy.

The difference between the Middle-Ages and the contemporary period is the fact that today a servant lives longer than a master.

Freedom is like the hanged-man's rope: if it is too short, it is useless.

Forgiveness is spiritual memory.

Good people are recognized by their soul and wicked people by their lack of it.

Bad news travels on horseback, good news on foot.

Like the pharaohs' tombs, our life is full of gold, but we do not know what to use it for.

Make your enemies your friends but tell them none of your secret!

Everything God punished in the Old Testament was forgiven by Jesus in the New Testament.

Don't contradict God! If you are right, you will regret.

Free verse poems are more sincere.

The Romanticism of the night is given by the Moon, while the splendour of the day is given by the Sun.

Above all God Almighty has to be God All-patient.

I don't expect anything from my enemies, they overload me with gifts.

If cockle did not grow in wheat fields, even lazy people would bake bread.

Longing is more intense than love, but it cannot procreate.

Impulse comes from the devil, restraint comes from saints.

The Sun believes the stars of the night bring about the bankruptcy of the sky.

The shadow of the peacock tail is uglier than the shadow of a boar head.

We snore only when we sleep without dreaming.

Life is a variable. Man is a constant.

Snow welds the earth and the sky.

The executioner's excuse "The sentence was not given by me."

If God and not Jesus had come down on earth, people would have crucified even Him.

Vanity is pride that has not been put to test.

I have been traveling to all the corners of the world and all of them seem round to me.

If fruit trees are beaten with a pole when their fruits are being picked up, they are no longer delighted to blossom.

The head is the menhir of the body.

Soldiers whose food ratio is increased, lose the war.

I am asking the saints to put in a good word for me with God, but they say nobody has done them this favour.

Boiled nettles do not sting anymore.

A wasp can sting, but it can't make honey.

If fruit trees bore fruit in spring, no one would take their time to admire the flowers.

A mother-in-law goes overboard on the wedding night and a wife on the very next day.

Some people live on cigarettes and I on thoughts.

Patience does not expect prizes.

I don't want you to tell me the truth. I want you to let me find it myself.

Grave diggers dig deeper graves for their enemies.

Never set off on a long journey on your own! Beware this is not an ad for cars.

If it does not hurt you when you bump against it, it means you have a greater pain.

You have good chances to win if you compete against those who are already in the race.

Mandrake is the flower on which not even dew drops will deposit.

The seven hills in Rome used to be the highest mountains.

Stop fighting! One cannot cut bread with a spear.

Weeds have given up on scent to avoid being picked up.

My solitude is collective, like New York's streets.

I am mad about life. In fact, life has maddened me.

Most people inhale the same air the others have exhaled.

I speak from my heart. I sometimes sound squeaky and some other times baritone like.

A writer is someone who suffers from Alzheimer and writes down his/her memoires.

On pay day all employees are hard working.

For some people a week has two weekends.

I am carrying my happiness in my arms as if it were a bride deflowered by someone else.

The devil is very proud of his Hell. He says it is more popular than Heaven.

It is very risky to love. It can become addictive.

Respect kills love.

A rotten apple spoils the others. A good apple doesn't restore any.

Believers' frequent mistake is that they ask God to give them things they will get in Heaven anyway.

Life is an opportunity you miss if you take advantage of it.

Waiting is a theft. It steals time necessary for other things.

Ancient gods used to share humans' vices. Nowadays people try to become as virtuous as God.

God let us free in Paradise. We should obey Him while we are alive.

If only kites knew doves are a symbol of peace!

No man is stronger than his/her ambitions.

It is better to see than to listen to a beautiful girl.

Who kills time kills their life.

You can die when you want, but you cannot live as long as you want.

The world is a Venetian mask parade: we keep smiling, but our legs are in water.

An oasis is lit through the reflection of the sun in the surrounding desert.

Don't ask a fallen man what pains him, help him to rise!

I was happier when I learnt to write than when I learnt to speak.

If you are stronger than your guardian angel, you are a sinner.

Our life story is read by God, browsed by angels, quoted by saints and put in a library by the devil.

If we have passion, we don't need a will.

We forgive because we forget. God forgives because He remembers.

Angels are more powerful when they come on earth. Humans are, too, but when they rise to heaven.

Gold merchants, no matter how much they get for it, are at a disadvantage.

Oases do not bring joy to Bedouins, because they confirm that the latter are still in the desert.

In a baker's shop you pray for your bread, in a church you pray for your fellow people's bread.

Hope is like a beautiful girl –it smiles at you from a distance.

Devils put on weight, angels get taller.

Christianity is exalted suffering.

Angels are the innocents of the Sky, the caregivers of the Heights.

The dog that wants in, is not a good guard.

The cat gets off the warm stove only for a bowl of cream.

A farmer's hands hide only his labor-chapped palms.

Law taken into one's own hands is called revenge.

Life begins and ends with a birth. The latter one is lasting.

Mankind was late for Plato's lectures on Philosophy. We attended only his evening classes called "The Dialogues".

Unhappiness is a waiting state. Happiness only reassures it.

The outer space flights fail because they cannot carry down to earth all the riches they come across.

How can Jesus go down on earth when people have flooded it with crosses?

Chauvinism is treble Darwinism.

Any man is more powerful than those who want to destroy him.

As we grow older, the mountains of our soul change into plains.

Whatever the Truth would say, lie still has something else to add to it.

We are the Salt of the Earth. Therefore, we dig it out of our body depth whenever we do something good.

Don't desert God on the dusty road only because the devil has a vacant seat in his carriage.

Eternity is the time you spend waiting.

Unlike the earth, the sky has no limits.

Today those who want to know what the future has in store for them no longer go to the oracle in Delphi. All they have to do is to count their money.

When you retire you add up your days off.

My moments of solitude started knowing each other.

When you expect nothing else from life any longer, life becomes bearable.

Magellan's discovery that the world is round, can somehow explain the cyclicity of evil.

The true extraordinary things happen to me when I sleep.

Memory is a bit Masochistic as it records failures first of all.

Who might love me, as I detest myself?

When saints quarrel, God is defeated.

Fallen angels are not those who no longer have wings, but those who no longer have a soul.

Only our internal happiness is unaltered.

God created the world and people divided it.

We grow up while we are getting closer to Death. We are so amazed at how much we have grown up, as is the Witch when she is looking at "Hansel and Gretel."

Death and Life are after the same thing, they both want to destroy us.

I keep telling my enemies: "Stop waiting for me! I am a long way ahead of you".

Just like Judah, all those I loved, want, now in the end, to kiss me.

How dangerous the mermaids would have been if they had been whole women!

Although bats lack brain, they oxygenate it constantly.

The plate, on which gods have put all the goodies for us, is within everybody's reach.

Indian sacred cow was milked by the English.

You may feel like leaving although you don't see the open door.

Eternity has nothing to do with longevity, on the contrary.

Divorce is suggested by one partner and accepted by both of them.

Angels without tiaras and wings are more credible.

If you take your part seriously, God is going to applaud your entire performance.

We usher our life out, like we usher someone to their grave.

It is ignoble to defeat the same enemy.

Good living destroys your life.

Barabbas has proclaimed himself King of the World, since he, and not Jesus, was chosen by the crowd.

People are some lightning rods through which angels are conducted to the ground.

I am a diligent student. I have got passing marks at all the retaken exams.

Even good people have nightmares.

Even if you are on holiday, you still have something to learn.

Do you want to be right? Contradict only your subordinates.

School is a labyrinth and if you want to find the way out, you have to answer all the questions they ask you.

I think that if Socrates were hired for a program called "We answer to our listeners", he would constantly be asking questions.

Active people measure time in minutes. Thinkers measure time in years.

The world is good only when it is seen from the outside.

The Devil is convinced that, without him, angels would not be highlighted.

A suffering man is still alive.

What we think about flying by plane, is what our soul thinks about transmigration, i.e. it is risky as it doesn't take us back where we started from.

Life is like a plugged electric appliance. The longer it functions, the warmer it gets, and it becomes more efficient.

When subordinates make suggestions, in fact, they give advice.

Religions which start from the serpent in the paradise allow people to enter their temples with their shoes on.

Tall temples house unfriendly gods.

Youth ends when you start paying attention to advice.

For many people, flavour is just something you have to spread on a slice of bread.

The man banished from the Garden of Eden is more like a snake's creation.

When people are pretty drunk, the party can go on without music.

Acknowledgement of victory is given only by the loser.

Victory laurels do not dry on anybody's forehead.

Parents are happier if their children grow taller than if they get an academic diploma.

How can a thought be a good thought when so many chemicals mediators give birth to it?

My heart has been hurt many times, but my coagulation is good.

Psychoanalytically, contraception makes a couple's love for their children grow.

Any panel is supposed to consist of experts, and thus its professionalism is compromised.

How powerful the untold words can be!

It is easier to climb a flourished mountain.

The black widow principle: when you are in love, you are already dead.

God does not consider Himself a creator, man does.

Any copyright is a second mark of Divinity.

Celebrity is like an edelweiss, everybody can see it, but no one is picking it.

One can get his peace of mind only on a battlefield.

I am like a minor civil servant –I get complete only if I am waiting.

One can see God's nail moving along the outline of a woman.

People are some peeping Toms. They enjoy insinuating themselves in everybody else's business.

I agree to die, but behind the undertakers' back.

Who keeps promises made while alive, tricks Death.

Life is a sad-ending comedy.

We ask a lot from God. God asks nothing from us. This is the false belief that God does not exist.

Even gods are sad. Therefore, sorrow is a privilege.

Anaerobic bacteria are superior to us. They live without oxygen.

Love is a figure of speech; therefore, artists feel its effects to the full.

I am copying my own thoughts. It is also a form of plagiarism.

Words are the feelings of traffic.

If you plucked a rose and you didn't bleed, then you did not choose the right one.

I have to guard some sorrows that would like to escape.

We praise God in order to prove how high we think of Him.

Golden apples are sweet even if they are crab-apples.

The world is so small that I feel useless.

How can I not feel lonely when all my friends are classics?

I have a good opinion about the people who detest me. They are down-to-earth people.

People who talk to themselves don't need a telephone anymore.

I speak all the languages of the world to find out which is the right one to make myself understood.

The real lucky guy is the one who knows that you will not strike luck tomorrow again.

Time is a prisoner in our time-measuring devices. That is why it takes revenge on us.

The motivation of the fight lies outside it. Therefore, it never ceases.

When angels go on strike, it is drought.

It is easy to detect cheaters at a gambling table. They don't rely on good luck.

Whoever describes Beauty has not seen it.

The dead who did not live their life have nothing to compare their Afterlife with.

For a righteous man Afterlife begins on earth.

The greatest happiness is when you defeat sorrow.

Wars bring fame to generals, and they can never be good peace negotiators.

The fish in the fishhook feels it is rising.

Although Mephisto bought Faust's soul, he has not become better.

When you are sad, you are the wittiest.

It is not difficult to climb the Mountain of Patience.

I am out in force, but the force is not mine.

How patient God is with us! He knows all our puerile intimacies.

We are building ice bridges. We are seasonal workers. We work only in winter.

Someone who has been yelling for a while can no longer sing.

My stomach seems full although I have had nothing to eat. Fasting works wonders.

Forgive me, my Lord! I feel I am wrong even when I am asking for forgiveness.

Optimists put off their hopes. Pessimists call them off.

Religion customizes Death. Philosophy makes Life miserable.

The devil wants only our body; therefore, he destroys our soul.

As I don't want to talk to a wall anymore, I have hung my friends' portraits on it.

It has been snowing for so long that our hair has grown under our hats.

People are the angels rejected by God.

Who believes death is near, should know it is already lurking.

Evil is the Devil unleashed.

Life is a trampoline. You are not propelled unless you stand against it.

We look at the sky meteorologically not theologically.

Soul is that part of us that wants to die. It is always willing to try new things.

Although water penetrates flint proving it is stronger, nothing can be built out of water.

God has not endowed us with wings, for fear we might leave the earth.

Priests pretend that God takes us seriously only inside a church.

Yells are the vocalizations of despair.

God takes you seriously when you offer, not when you ask.

God is waiting for us in Heaven, and we have houses built on earth.

God has asked us to love each other, and we manufacture contraceptives.

Believers have several gods. Sinners have only one devil.

After you die, you can go to God only if you know already His address.

I have not succeeded in counting nine out of the ten Biblical beatitudes.

Be afraid only of the final prophecies!

In religion people defy death through emotions.

The angel has come alive. The icon seems to be moving.

Heavy words fall into our souls like stones into an ostrich stomach.

Who can postpone a fight already humiliates their opponent.

Your happiness is unfair for the unhappy.

My life is a novel written in a foreign language.

We live in a cave. Who is in charge with painting the walls is going to enter history.

God urges you to get to Him, not to die.

A true champion does not look back, only ahead, where he can see nobody else.

A raisin is the mummy of the wine.

We are the champions of the same flaws.

If Columbus had known he would reach America, he would have taken some dollars with him.

Angels speak out of God's beard.

Life is an accident. Death is not.

How clear the sky is after a storm! That is why the optimists call forth the clouds.

Three full stops indicate three missing phrases.

No country is stronger than the others. Perhaps more cultured.

I am a pacifist. I am fighting only with angels.

A vesper is the funeral service of a day.

Don't make way for your enemy or else you will be made to join their army!

In a world full of sorrow, clowns rely mostly on make-up.

What a perfect symbiosis is there between happiness and unhappiness in a passive man!

No other language is more beautiful than your mother tongue!

Like any other earthquake, I limit myself to disasters.

I feel well on my own. Just like Jesus on the Cross!

A visible angel would not be able to fly.

Scholars recreate the World; whereas, the devil is pleased with experiments.

The events that have marked my life, came from inside.

Saints' voices sound like God's voice.

Life is ordinary. Intrigues are all that matters.

Lucifer is the only angel who has realized God does not exist.

Prizes of fidelity should not be awarded. Fidelity and prize awarding exclude each other.

Beauty evaluated on aesthetic criteria is getting obsolete.

Summer and spring are alike, but in summer flowers start bearing fruits.

No bee thinks honey is sweet.

A feeling, that becomes an impulse, denies its divine nature.

Since cannibalism is a thing of the past, people have been eating each other.

People are good, but only as separate individuals.

Who does not believe in God, denies his/her own Father.

My thoughts are my hare legs.

Mephisto is an incurable pessimist. Whatever happens to him is transferred to the entire world.

The world is an alternative curse.

In life only those who do not hitch their wagon to a star are successful, but they are successful from their own point of view.

Churches are painted till painters get to the first layer of angels.

The world is perfect but only theoretically.

I am my own life's guardian angel.

I am playing chess with God. The devil is approaching us holding a backgammon board under his arm.

I am paying a fortune for my insanity.

After Life is a sublimation of this current one.

Mediocre people think success is not about winning but about not being defeated.

The more devastating a volcano eruption is, the more spectacular it will be.

I am half angel, half human. My human half is inferior.

Ambition requires, first of all, a good memory.

Burning embers are more powerful than the fire they start, but they cannot be consumed by it.

A woman's masculinity is not only about clitoris.

The most powerful people are those who stay.

A world seized by crisis, does not regard bankruptcy a solution.

Peasants come from history on foot.

A dog with a bone in its mouth cannot protect you.

Bosses are covered in lint.

What crises of personality martyrs have!
If you watch a tragedy, you shed tears and even if you don't, you still cry.

If you just beg your enemy to leave you alone, he/she won't do it.

We would not be so serene when we leave if we were not sure, we would return.

Marriage is a spiritual exchange.

The real winner is the one who fights.

The World is the upside-down Sky.

Premonitions are like good ideas: when you have them, it is too late.

No one is braver than a man who succeeded in defeating his own fear.

God loves us like a father because He values us.

Sick people welcome their death.

Life is a zigzag journey. Those who go straight ahead are always left aside.

People love at night, because daylight makes them look ugly.

God does not need wings. Angels do.

I am in the middle of a difficult period of time. I enjoy living.

Perfection is supreme routine process.

A racing horse loses a derby when it gets used to the riding-crops.

The more I write, the less I read, and therefore I become less cultivated.

Enemies keep me fit.

The true Dao is not the way but the method.

For all non-Christian religions, I am a heretic.

Ask for your rights only from someone who is more powerful than you.

Coffee would not be poured into a cup if it weren't drunk hot.

I cultivate my feelings like a gardener that cultivates flowers.

Buds are so patient because they are waiting for their fruits.

A dog in a butcher's shop doesn't leave, but it doesn't live long either.

I am walking on a wire that is stretched on the ground.

A man is stronger than his guardian angel.

Walk around the world! Otherwise, you will admire only the vehicle you will travel by.

The more protected the truth is, the purer.

I am cultivating water lilies in my spiritual marshes.

A sunrise sacrifices the night show for the Moon's sake.

After we plough the land, the dead can breathe better.

I am voting for my despair, raising my both hands to the Sky.

A lion with no mane would be chased by dog catchers, and not safari hunters.

Celebrity is like music: you can hear it in the room where it is sung/ played but they talk about it everywhere.

Even after guillotine was abolished, a lot of heads kept falling.

God prefers me to angels or else He would not ask me to do so many chores.

Fight with your enemies, or else they may become your friends!

The guardian angel is the indispensable electronic orbital of each and every one of us.
Evil is everywhere, that is why Good is so feeble.

I have a lot of friends among priests. My family isn't going to pay much for my funeral.

If all good people die, who will God rely on in this world?

Merchants think about profit. Workers think about damage.

The dead are not in the ground, they are in Heaven. Only their bodies are in the ground.

Stars are the sky's measles.

Although the saints' bodies are meagre, they hold the world so well.

Metaphysically a day in Heaven is more expensive than a day on earth.

The foot in the grave is the supportive foot.

God is the poor impresario of our destinies.

No matter how much we may be disappointed by the other people, we disappoint ourselves more.

The real world is parallel to the imaginary world. According to superior non-Euclidean geometries, the two worlds should meet in Heaven's Infinite.

The real melancholy is the longing for what has not happened yet.

There is so much melancholy in us, that "past tense" is called "perfect tense" in grammar rigor.

A true bullfighter does not enter an arena the moment the bull is dead, no matter how much he is being cheered.

Night is more beautiful than all the women you may have in your bed throughout its length.

I am so intransigent that my heart has asked for political asylum.

If you vote by raising both your hands, you won't increase its value, you will annul it.

We are ready to do whatever it takes to die old.

The happiness we can anticipate is tedious.

Love in excess leads to twins.

Rose thorns become invisible because of their scent.

A woman keeps a house whose architect is a man.

He has such a hulky body and such a small soul!

When you are saying: "Allow me to tell you the truth" you are already an impostor.

Smuggled merchandise is several times cheaper.

A snail is vulnerable with or without its shell.

I wonder what wood essence Pinocchio's nose was made of, that could grow any time he told a lie? Such a tree would be a good forestry investment.

Ambition is a wicked will.

It takes you nine months to give birth to a child, nine years to educate it and twenty years to see whether you have succeeded.

Failure used to signify waiting for something, but gradually it has lost its patience.

There are so many feathers all over my body. The Good Angel and the Bad Angel have fought against each other again.

The body is full only after three courses. The soul is full just by looking at the dessert.

Just like in the shows performed in fairs, the soul handles the body from inside.

If you admit your mistake before making it, you make it seem bigger.

The birds that do not sing in spring are autochthonous.

The child that inherits your assets is the same one who has stolen your walking stick.

The progress towards the current is called drift.

Cattle lick salt and lions the blood on their necks.

The more admired a flower is, the more violently it is plucked from its root.

Who has the capacity of foreseeing the future, does not hurry anymore.

Lay the weapons down, and you will have the opportunity to hug each other.

Faith is like a flower. If you say you have it, it means you have plucked it so as to show it to everybody.

God does not come when you call for Him, He comes when you are praying.

People who do not trust the words of the Bible are less cultured than those who are illiterate.

Jesus wore the thorn crown on His forehead. We wear ours in our soul.

All earthly loves have been illegitimate since Zeus.

The older a proverb, the fresher!

If we lie like truth, when we tell the truth we will compromise it.

If the Moon had the brightness of the Sun, it would not be surrounded by so many stars.

Mediocre people are the champions of statistics.

Prostitutes have enormous resources of love, but they misdirect them. That is why Maria Magdalena has become a saint.

Don't worry! The true enemies will never leave you.

Life is a piece of glazed smoked meat.

My love, I would like to continue writing to you, but I have run out of stamps.

If I were not a man, I would like to be a woman.

There are women, young people and senior people world organizations. Only mature men have no complex.

Daydreams are less credible than night dreams.

An evil man is like wormwood. He is looking for some wine to make it bitter.

The post coach of love does not stop.

The bridal veils hide a few brides' emotion and the infidelity of most of them.

The water in tears belongs to lacrimal gland. The salt in tears belongs to soul.

I appreciate my girlfriends in the order of their appearance.

A camel that crosses the desert comes across an oasis. A man that crosses the desert comes across God.

The heart looks at freedom through the rib grid.

How complex a vampire blood group must be!

Goddess Venus is incriminated more than she should be, because a part of venereal diseases are transmitted by men.

If the employer does not work, the employees think it is a banking holiday.

I have caught a cold. The coldness started from my soul.

Geniuses become famous posthumously, celebrities become famous before birth.

I am writing -the same way I am wearing my double-breasted suit-in double rows.

The law of retaliation – I love you so you must love me.

Who does not have the courage to examine the truth, has not understood its essence.

Pindar was defeated in a poetry contest by a beautiful woman. The panel appreciated face aesthetics.

To have patience one needs courage. Courage manifests itself only when patience disappears.

The world is not as rich as it used to be when God created it, but neither is it as poor as it might have been after the devil plundered it.

When you are in front of God only if you kneel, you are as tall as you can be.

The beadrolls are written for the priests. God knows our kin.

If a writer's hands are not tied behind his back, he is free.

The deeper the water in the well is, the bigger the fish grows.

Mini -skirted and low-necked women take photos, even if they are not photo -reporters.

The ideal world is a no-direct-neighbour Polynesia.

One doesn't have to ask God to love them. It is like asking money for food from the Earth. It wouldn't have starved you out anyway.

How perfect the sunshine gets into our soul and how distorted the shadows of the body are!

But for the body, the soul would be pristine.

The real solitude is when you miss the others.

In the cemetery of our actions the righteous ones have no cross.

The very moment you accept your Destiny it changes.

One single good deed, and slander is gone.

Only the Pearly Gates are guarded by Saint Peter, the Hell Gates are wide open.

The ashes that cannot catch fire again can put out the cleansing fire.

In God's eyes nothing can be more important than a person. Personality is the empty emancipation of a person.

Arrogance is the pemphigus of an individual.

Borrowed money is spent faster than earned money.

I am a slave. My shackles are with God.

I have never been on exile. I don't think it is a beautiful country.

I blame myself. I have never been in favour of blaming the others.

While you are waiting for someone, in your mind they have already arrived.

Don't lend your soul! Nobody gives it back intact.

Gold glitters in the darkness of the mountains.

Death does not sever life. It is its continuation.

The only regret of a believer is that once he/she doubted.

Only fishers admire the lakes.

Faith is the meeting between your thought about God and His thought about you.

Faith is to be in Heaven while still acting on Earth.

Faith is the good thought carried out when we do something right.

Faith without doubt is ideology.

Believing is more than hoping because it includes carrying it into action.

The weaker your faith is the farther from you God is.

A believer is like anybody else, but he/she is one of God's people.

Faith increases in church, but it is proved outside it.

Faith is like gravitational force. It is in us, but it comes from outside.

Those who repeat a school year are the most diligent. They review the material several times.

Life is a beautiful Lipovan woman, who takes her drink. If the drink is on you, you get drunk under the table first.

The Star of my Birth disintegrated into stratosphere. I am charged with being still alive by the ecologists.

Death is a one-stop bus whose doors don't open between stops.

The worm in the apple is subtler than the serpent because it tempts you to eat the apple.

Don't shake the fruit trees! When the fruits get ripe, they all fall.

I am so alien to me that I have edited my own dictionary.

"I would like to die", but only my sick organs say it.

God makes a concession to artists when He allows them to beat about the bush and tell lies like truth.

Hell has central heating, and they don't cease working in winter.

I am a dead man like all the others, but when I was alive, I looked like nobody else.

Bad speakers are also bad listeners.

The forests have been destroyed not because of the libraries, but because of our constant sensation of cold.

World crisis first traversed me.

I am an ordinary mortal; therefore, I am reluctant when it comes to showing my wings to you.

The appetite we live with, disgusts the grave diggers.

My face is on the covers of my books for the readers to know who they deal with.

For some people a detective story is more thrilling than the Bible. It is the difference between decoded and revealed truth.

Angels are concerned whether they have a body. We are concerned whether they have a gender.

The general stands in front of the army only at peace.

In winter I am the man who has gone to pick wild strawberries because his girlfriend has used them all to make pancakes.

I am the label on a wine bottle. If you keep me it means you have liked me.

The North Star points to the north. Not all sailors want to sail north, though.

Since I was a child, I have been looking for God. When I got older, I found Him and asked Him to make me a child again. "But you are going to lose me again", said God.

All religions borrow ideas. Christianity gives to charity.

When I tell a lie I am as convincing as Baron of Munhaunsen, I do it so arduously that I believe myself.

A pack of wolves does not need a shepherd. A flock of sheep does.

God has created the world from nothing. One cannot stake a claim to such material.

Humans are so proud that they get upset if another human, not God, answers to their prayer.

Agreement is global, consent is individual.

Aladdin's lamp stands for tradition. Something old is more expensive than something new.

Immediate reality can convince us so well, that those scholars who rely on it fail their theories.

God is waiting. The Devil is here already.

Waiting relies on time. Arriving relies on a second.

Life is a drama of passage.

I was born in computer era. The only man who used his brains was Bill Gates.

Desire is erotic longing.

It was not Pan's panpipe that played havoc, it was what he did when he stopped playing it.

Some people have a weapon license, some others a library license.

Believers worship mainly the saint perched on the church fence and who stands guard to announce them when God comes.

I am talking in my sleep. I have made some progress. Now I am dreaming sonorously.

Merchants hold down the world's evolution. They sell what they have bought.

The difference between our working week and God's working week when he created the world, is that he did something else every day.

Women who dress up and put on make-up in order to be loved, give false clues. They make people who might love them, pay attention to the result of their transformation.

Art's role is to make us happy. Art succumbs when happiness arrives. All artists are unhappy.

A philosopher dies every day. A Christian dies every second.

 Socrates died in order to show us how ignoble it is to be mortal. Jesus died in order to show us the dignity of immortal condition.

Our mother loves us till the age of twenty. She supports us till the age of forty. She commiserates us all the time thereafter.

Oedipus was wrong, not because he loved his mother. He was wrong because he loved her physically.

What a paradox. I am asking my destiny not to knock me out, so I can see who the winner is.

Theseus was saved by Ariadna's thread. It means going together on the same road on which his beloved had walked before. Love is the escape from the Labyrinth, the sacrifice of one of the partners, the one who had initiated the journey and had gone on scouts in order to provide the opportunity for the other to be saved.

A human is more afraid of his own death than he is of the Apocalypse. His problem is the fact that many people will outlive him.

God said, "Come up to the sky" The pilots were the first to get His message.

Iago could not have been accepted in Romeo and Juliet's tragedy. When you are 13 or 17 love is pure. Juliet did not cry in her hanky and Romeo did not need subordinates.

The old man's daughter, in the tale is kind-hearted. The widowed father's daughter, Cinderella, is kind –hearted, too. Cruelty is inherited from our mother, but the greatest kindness comes from her, too.

Being concerned about dying does not absolve you of its consequences.

Jesus did not live long. The Man had to die in order to make room for God.

Man has several degrees of solitude, as electrodes have different degrees of freedom chronologically, they are the following: the first degree, useful solitude is called books. The second degree, entertainment solitude, is called TV, the third degree, addictive drug–like solitude, is called computer.

Do we want to be alone? All we need is a key. Do we want to be with someone? All the phones in the world are not enough.

He who loves only what he sees is sentenced to lose all his loves.

When the separation is painful it is advisable that you should go on foot so you can hear if you are called back.

You can do almost anything against your will, but you cannot help loving. Therefore, love is the only genuine feeling in us.

I am competing with the crickets. They sing better, I am lazier.

Money does not change anyone it changes only their condition.

If the Three Magi had brought such gifts as gold, myrrh and frankincense into the house of some ordinary people, they would have been given thanks only for the gold.

Wise people ask questions. The others are ready with the answers.

If you are a man on Earth, God is going to make you a saint in heaven.

God appreciates His creation in us, but more than that He appreciates our own creation.

We do not work our own salvation if we get rid even of love.

When God hurt Adam he fractured one of his ribs.

A lot of people would rather live a new life on Earth than live eternally in Heaven.

God cannot be lied. A priest can. That is why there is confessions.

You cannot be a hero every day. But you can try being one till you succeed.

Billionaires do not have money, they have accounts.

God does not advise. He guides.

We absolve our fellow people from those sins that are ours.

Be amazed, as the crowd was, when they saw Jesus, but do not crucify the Miracle.

On the way to virtue, people do not meet with each other because they walk ahead with equal strides.

Truth is criticism, but if it does not include the one who tells it, then it is dissimulated.

When your will gets tired, it calls impotence to its assistance.

Lie is happy when Truth is misunderstood, and the former comes up with explanations.

The more saints hang around, the closer to the mountain peak the monastery is.

In grammar and in life, perfect is just a past tense.

I am a pearl diver. Although I have found none, I have realized how wonderful the ocean is.

Each of us is the martyr of our own life. We become real martyrs only when we become the martyrs of other people's life.

The piece of God in us is larger than that piece of God left behind in Heaven.

Death has looked for me several times, but my enemies, thinking they can hurt me by doing it, told it I had died a long time ago.

I have asked people to listen to me, and they started recording my conversations.

God has promised His world to us because He knows we have spoilt ours irreversibly.

On Doomsday God will call us to be forgiven.

Death is such a common daily fact. We experience it whenever our soul is asleep.

To be God's servant, that is perfect freedom.

Pot flowers do not need spring any longer.

Insanity is the thought that you have recovered from it.

Stupidity is a large country. It is so large that you cannot roam it on your own.

We are unhappy because of what happens to us and happy because of what could happen to us.

We live in a cage whose door opens only when bad weather slams it open, but we do not dare to get out.

The compassionate man gives you alms while the stingy man counts your courses.

In vain do you have a square meal if there is no one you can share it with.

On realizing God made us from clay, some people hurried to make their heart from stone.

Distributivity principle: God loves us more than we love each other.

To want is more difficult than to be able to.

The journey to God starts at the back of your house.

In the Palace of Eternity there are no measuring time devices.

History looks back, and minimizes, Politics looks ahead, and amplifies.

The shoulder blades are angel wings that have become atavistic for not having been used.

Embryo is an egg with no shell.

We are satisfied with little. We are choosy compared to the people who are pleased even when they get nothing.

If we start with the wings, we become pilots not angels.

When you work on your free days, the effort is half, and the pay is double.

God calls you to church, but He asks you to do a few good deeds on your way to it.

A dream that has come true is useless when the dreamer has a new one.

Happiness is like a flower petal. Both sunshine and rain can spoil it.

The lesson of the Flood: It is better to make a new world than to change the existing one.

A lion without its mane is only a bailiff in the jungle.

A soldier killed in action cannot stand when he is being saluted.

Having been created by God, man went on to deny Him.

Nature can still be beautiful without being admired while a woman cannot.

History wants you to be eternal. Politics wants you to be out in large number.

The Devil works for a woman, and she wants him to pay her.

The Devil is upset because you do not call him emperor.

A fly in a beehive is covered in honey. Nevertheless, it does not notice the latter's hard work.

The confrere of a hard-working bee is a lazy bumble bee.

The eyes are on the front of your head so you cannot look back.

A sin enters stealthily because it has been speeding for long.

Boiled wine still intoxicates.

Don't trust a man after he has eaten but listen to a man after he has drunk.

A man and his shadow come together.

A thief can hide but his shadow on the wall gives him away.

An angel whom God calls to him too many times, may believe he is Saint Peter.

When they speak about orgies in Heaven, Saint Peter says he cannot guard the gates and see what is happening inside at the same time.

When temptation besieges the soul, virtues feed the latter so it can resist.

First God created the world, then He created us, as He didn't want us to feel lonely.

God has offered us His Heaven and we played havoc with His apples.

No spring lasts longer than its flowers.

We are living not mortal beings.

Moments of solitudes are concentric One no longer exists in the deepest circle.

Roots can never see the splendour of the fruit they feed.

An explanation is the dead end to a solution. Who has ever calculated the number of free days a novelist needs in order to write his/her novels?

Glory is inner pride.

We are not God's slaves, we are His servants. Bondage implies voluntary servitude that is sealed with overwhelming love.

We ask from God more than what He asks from us.

God is the perfect institutional pattern and anybody's access to Him is conditioned only by love and respect.

If frogs did not croak, herons would not catch them.

Parents who spoil their children when they attend a school meeting hold teachers to account.

God has created only one man. We are just copies of the original.

God has warned us that He cannot banish us anywhere beyond This World.

Linden trees are more scented than apple trees, but they do not bear fruit.

Honesty, courage and high boots must be tried on.

In a herbarium even weeds are appreciated.

One can remove the weeds from earth, but no one can remove the crows from the sky.

A journey can be backwards or forwards depending on which direction you look.

The world is a sailing ship. All species with the exception of Noah are allowed onboard.

The Flood was the baptism of the world, and the mass of water was so huge that it was a match for the serious sins of everyone on earth.

The road from man to God is covered with brambles while the road from God to man is covered with flowers.

There is only one God and an inflation of believers.

God comes but He cannot stay as long as you want Him to.

God created the world, and the devil claims he polishes it.

The future looks like the past —only the people who live in it are different.

God has given us a day off, i.e., Sunday, and we are looking for Him to ask Him why.

Since a dessert is not so healthy you have it at the end of a meal when you are already full.

Doomsday is too tough. You cannot repent then.

When angels fall, they fall into hell, not onto earth.

The scholars who give different answers to the same question have not agreed on technology yet.

Waiting is full of hope bur hope avoids waiting.

The mad man admits he is crazy about anything.

Eminescu is not a genius poet. He is the genius.

Don t buy an ox before the yoke, the ox might die before you get the yoke.

It is difficult to hoe
Before the sun to bed does go
It is easier to eat
Before the sun decides "to quit"

A fox, even when in disguise, displays its tail.

A crow, even dead, scratches with its claws.

I work because I want to have, not because I want to be praised.

If a fish bumps into the glass of the aquarium may believe the low tide has come.

Saint Peter's dilemma: If God forgives all the sinners, then why has he appointed him to guard the Heaven's Gate?

I told my enemies "If I weren't so romantic, I would have slapped you"

Sweethearts are like money: the more you have the more tempted you feel not to take pride in them.

When sporting fishing was replaced with industrial fishing, the fishing rod was replaced with the fishing net.

The angels in Heaven have lost their sleep since Newton discovered the Law of Gravitation.

Any point is twice farther from us than it seems because we have to calculate the return distance as well.

I am the cultural waiter of your life, so: "What would you like to have?"

You may think you cheated on a great scammer whose playing cards were doctored but you will find out that his/her money was forged.

A real hero is both defeated and unsung. He dies with this attenuation induced by glory and success.

In vain do you swim in fresh water when you are thirsty if you do not get drowned a little.

I represent all the people who died when they were my age.

You are first baptized in the amniotic fluid, the second time in your mother's kisses and the third time in the Jordan.

When you die, you do not have the chance to bid farewell to all the people. Anyway, you will soon meet with them again.

Indulgence means accepting that weeds are flowers, too.

The headings "Did you know that..." impress because they give a conclusion lacking the preceding stages, the dull and complicated research leading to them. Thus fascinating, spontaneous people who introduce to us only such singularities and erudite platitudes impose themselves.

Life has both bad solutions and miraculous salvations.

Saints are people whom God called to Him and who come a bit late, after performing some unfinished good actions.

Dream is hope's hallucination. A plan is its theorization.

Heaven is not the place where we are waited for us after death, it is the place we are building to go to, after death.

We are not loved according to our qualities, but according to the loving capacity of those who care about us.

No woman takes off enough of her clothes if she is not sincere.

Will is unfettered body, love is unfettered heart and madness is unfettered mind.

A philosopher does not know why he/she loves, and someone in love does not know who he/she loves.

Faustus sold his soul to Mephistos and posterity forgave him. Judah sold Jesus to the Romans, and he has been blamed ever since. One can do whatever he/she wants with his/her soul. No one has control over someone else's soul.

We pray to saints but, in fact, we have God in mind.

If someone wishes you a long life, they must have seen in you a possible support for them.

Suicide is to burst into the afterlife without being invited.

Lawyers make justice for the people who have taken the law into their own hands.

Symmetry creates beauty and destroys the spirit.

Angels bring only good news. Evil is not part of the divine plan. It is accidental and catastrophic and cannot be envisioned.

Success that depends on circumstances, just like the money in the treasury, is not yours. You know to whom it belongs but if you take it, it is still a theft.

I am a day-labourer of my own life.

Memory is the reminiscence of the past.

God is in everything around us. We are getting deeper and deeper into His soul with every step we take towards Him.

I am like a banker. I know all the money I have is not mine.

If we eat and dream every day, we must also read every day.

Nothing impresses me more than a blank sheet of paper.

I educate my destiny to understand that it belongs only to me.

A good chef changes a house special to please their customer.

There are more flies than bees in honey.

I cannot be on my own willingly. Therefore, I have to use a key.

All my accomplishments have been un-commercial.

When I fall in love I will announce the court registry.

Wasps make venom. Bees make honey.

A lot of people have been trampled down during peace rallies.

It is God, not the priests, who gives us His blessings.

The advantage of water lilies is that they are water flowers, and they never wither.

Solitude is the only training that exhausts us.

Shadow is what a body understands of Sunshine. Eyesight is what soul does of it.

When an enemy comes to you and asks for reconciliation, don't ask him/her why he /she is doing it, ask him/her how long it will last.

A root never sees the superb flower it feeds.

To give up on hopes means giving up on the most beautiful part of one's future.

Anaesthetics take your pain away, but they also prevent you from feeling a tender caress.

A bitch raises its tail even when it meets a castrated dog.

Men measure the depth of a barrel using a mug.

A butler who performs all his duties gets on his master's nerves.

Unlike most body pathological diseases, all soul diseases are transmissible.

Soul can be healed negotiating with the disease.

If only one single girlfriend loved me like my mother does, I would make a child like me with her.

I am preaching culture. I am like those football fans who come back from the stadium carrying their portable transistors on full volume.

I can read between the lines. I mean between the blank lines. My imagination is total.

I am exiling in me. What a sweet banishment!

The charm of a garden is given by its flowers.

Good people fall in love fast.

Do not ask a lawyer what justice is for he will make you produce witnesses!

God does not come down for all the gold in the altar, but he does it when a beggar kneels down.

Salinity cleans sea water, but it also makes it undrinkable.

A woman looks at herself in the mirror more often than she looks at her husband.

Whatever a woman puts on, a man takes off.

Glory is the disappointment of virtue.

The dust on Roman sandals is Greek.

I am coming back, my love, from my way to glory, to look at you-just like a wolf chasing a deer, I am coming back altogether.

There is no one else I can sacrifice but myself.

There is concrete in the clepsydra of geniuses.

While alive our life is measured in years. Posterity measures it in actions.

Destiny is not what happens to you. It is what happens to you unintentionally, by chance.

My poor soul, you want to love, and your body gets in first.

The head of a pin keeps the pin thrust.

There was a little hemlock left in Socrates' cup but there were not other philosophers willing to speak so openly and accusingly in public places, so as to educate the young people and defy the gods.

The Gold Rush brought about the permanent Time Rush.

I am sacrificing my life, but not my death.

I have some dirt in my shoes. I want to cultivate myself.

One can truly defeat the night if they sleep at night.

David and Goliath would have had equal chances in their fight if David had been bigger.

We are animated by so much a vital hope. No one saves their first salary or their first pension to spend it for their funerals.

Shame is sadness of not being able to say what you feel.

The sun needs clouds more than the Earth does.

A lot of people may be those who are unhappy, but most of them seem to have crossed the threshold of my house.

Life is a snake that loses its skin without growing a new one instead.

 There are fewer than three-hundred and sixty-five days in celebrities' calendar.

During the day I am obsessed with the night's dreams and at night with day's realities.

Enemies examine you more thoroughly than your friends. They are your most objective critics.

If snowdrops did not pierce the snow where no other flower could grow without sacrificing itself, they would not be called spring's heralds.

When someone comes back from exile, they love even the dust of their homeland.

No other fruit is as savoury as grapes, but this is a viticulturist's opinion.

Relatives are blood enemies.

The most valuable is a blank bank check.

When atheists are afraid, they cross themselves with their tongue not to be seen.

When our guardian angel has to face the mud in us, he do not hesitate to dirty his white wings.

Sire, but for your crown who would be following you?

Sigh is despair's breath.

My enemies are wearing boxing gloves when they deal with me.

But for the Sun even the shadows would vanish.

I am going counter clockwise to save time.

I am selling my soul to the Devil hoping to meet Faust's

The dead are sceptical and refuse to sign wills anymore.

The prudent husband gets himself a mistress before he gets married.

Democracy sacrifices individual freedom for collective freedom.

The Greeks used to worship the Mount Olympus, the Jews used to worship the whole sky.

Soul can get well in a simple way. It negotiates the illness again.

Humanity is feminine pride.

The hero who heard the victory news is not impressed when he hears the death news.

Not all those who come back halfway are cowards. Half of them are forgetful.

## AMBITION

Ambition turned into pride can no longer give up on this title.

Ambition is implemented hope.

Ambition is the arrogance of hope.

When we say it is easy to do something we are determined to overcome difficulties.

My ambition has taken all my passions seriously.

Vanity is unjustified ambition.

Progress is how time succeeds in satisfying our ambitions.

Fatigue is ambition assessing its results.

Napoleon used to say that "Impossible" is not a French word. I believe no other language is willing to claim this word.

## ANGELS

I am like an angel. I keep flying up to the sky without reaching my destination, though.

I am a multiple-personality angel.

Angels are the redemption. They have wings and can fly, but they cannot cross themselves.

The fact that angels come from the Sky, does not provide them with an excuse for their falling.

We are the angels of a leaning Sky. Any hesitation in front of Kindness takes us down.

Unlike angels, birds are happy they have wings, at least for the mating period.

Angels show us that although they have wings, body is not enough if we want to ascend.

Angels would not be able to fly if they will not. If they were ambitious, they would overthrow God.

The Russian astronauts complained they did not see any angels in the sky. How could they if they were still alive.

Humans are angels that hired their wings.

If you start a day well, it means that during the night an angel has guarded you.

## APPRECIATIONS

I am admirable, but not admired.

Our merit is always appreciated by others.

A prize always postpones new achievements.

Critics are afraid to praise. They are like some obese people who are afraid to eat a good dessert.

Respect relies on force that is stimulated at a certain moment.

Those who respect us have a divine perspective on us.

Any prize is a fidelity prize.

Envy is admiration that has lost its spontaneity.

Respect is the thought that you may become worthy of it.

We treasure everything that deserves being treasured but when it is too late.

## ART

Art is the insanity of coding your mistakes.

Art is culture display.

All art masterpieces are old, thus any deficiency they may display is attributed to time. Venus of Milo may have had male hands.

Art overloads nature in an obvious way. If we painted some waves on a dam, it would be ridiculous. The mermaid on the seashore, the symbol of Denmark, by Andersen is perfectly integrated in the environment. It is the unreal washed by real waters. On one hand it does not disturb nature tautologically, as it does not belong to it, and on the other hand it brings a fairy tale into the true light of tangibility.

Talent does not improve a work of art, but it makes it more acceptable

Art is Proust's telegram where an explicative lie is superfluous nowadays. Each reader has to invent it himself. Umberto Eco names this work that amplifies itself ad infinitum, an "open work".

Hermetic Art is angelic, it is a kind of chastity that reveals itself only to a few initiated, and God can be seen in the light, only after we say our prayer.

In art ugly is beautiful. Monsters painted by Goya used to adorn his house, while the hungry monsters by Rabelais became allegorical educative parables. It is more difficult to handle ugliness than to represent beauty since beauty is sufficient in itself. Ugliness transgresses, gives hints about the other side, defines through its opposite. In the Empire of Ugliness, the artist becomes a

Jesus figure, who rises from Golgotha, the Mount of Garbage. It is blasphemed to rise from the Mount of Olives.

Just like Hamlet any artist pretends to be insane within their work. They do not take sides with any of their characters, keeping a Chekhovian neutrality.

Insanity is not pathological, it is luminous aiming at a cognition whose significations are intentionally detached.
The paradox of this lunatic state is the awakening in the art fan, of lucidity and conviction that Figaro cannot make fun of the things he does not understand.

An aesthetician does not have to admire beauty, he has to notice it. If you contemplate it, if you are captivated by it, this is a limitation or an imposed targeting which contravenes to a critic's deontology.

How little imagination the artists have! All their creations will finally become reality.

The first art gallery consisted of cave paintings.

Paintings are hatched lines.

## BEAUTY

Beauty is the most faithful sandglass.

When we get old our eyesight gets weak, so we notice only partially the diminution of beauty.

Of all types of beauty, only feminine beauty descends directly from Genesis.

A man meets a lot of beautiful women in his life. Unfortunately, none of them finds him handsome.

My beauty is skin deep that is why I have never participated in any beauty contest.

In the world of man there is beauty even among mushrooms, but bright colours sometimes signalize danger.

The flowers we do not picked will bloom for us.

Sun rays which do not reach our soul wrinkles our face.

I have mirrored myself in a dewdrop and I liked how I would have looked like if I had been a flower.

The zephyr rings in the snowdrops' bells and announces spring.

We are some cannibals of beauty and without hesitation we eat the flowers turned into fruits.

"My sweetheart, I admire you as I admired the desert when I crossed it, holding live water in my cupped hands. However, I didn't touch the water because I forgot about it".

"You, caterpillars if you keep on drinking the dew you will choke on beauty".

My eyes are beautiful for I have seen a lot of sensitive faces.

Every day the sea waves ask me to build some new sand structures for them.

"You are as beautiful as my mother. Rejoice because I have never paid this compliment before."

You cannot embellish a meadow with picked flowers.

## THE BIBLE

The Bible is a colour book that you have to draw for if you don't, its reading is useless.

I'd better read the Bible than paraphrase God.

God has offered us a book, the Bible, so we can be altar high, but instead we started reading it.

Slogans are those verses not included in the Bible.

## TRUTH

If you asked me to tell you the truth, I would do it. As you don't do it, I am writing it to you.

Truth is the edelweiss of reality.

If we told what had happened to us only those who took us at our word, we would be elliptical.

A writer writes for those who don't believe him/her.
If you are the only one who has perceived the truth, when you tell it, you are not believed, as it seems to be a lie.

Truth is not upset when lie tells it that it has not understood a word.

You can't lie unless you know the truth.

Only the unknown truth fails to express itself.

Exposed lies become means of finding out the truth.

You cannot hide yourself in front of nature.

Convicts know that truth does not set them free.

No matter how honest the truth may be, there are a lot of lies that succeed in conceiving illegitimate children using it.

Whatever is beautiful it is beautiful because it is true.

Truth would die if lie did not resuscitate it by slapping it.

We eat as we lie, with our mouth wide open. How long can you, my Soul, resist?

If you say something true, one thousand liars, around you, would let you move on.

Truth looks great when naked.

The echo of truth resounds from the abyss of uncertainties.

The truth that does not resist any questions, loses its crown.

If truth didn't hurt, it would not be felt.

The only defeat that makes us famous is the defeat of truth.

The real winners are those who know, before the fight begins, what they are going to win.

When truth touches you, it appeals to lie.

We may repeat the truth as often as we like, but it will not become a slogan.

It is equally dangerous both to tell the truth and to reject it.

The truth we tell and the truth we are afraid to understand are the same.

The Christian name of realness is truth.

Reality exists. Truth has to be discovered.

Any explanation given for the truth distorts it.

When truth does not help you in any way, you learn how to lie.

I am the truth for which I cannot find an explanation.

How much truth is there in the unuttered truth!

The truth about us can be found out, only if we disguise ourselves.

Truth is how reality blames us.

A truth that does not hurt is like champagne without effervescence.

Whatever they say about us is true as long as it is not us who say it.

The existence of truth is undermined by any concession.

A lot of lies are served at truth's table and everybody turns a blind eye.

On your fast- moving journey to truth, you come across a lot of lies tempting you make a halt.

Truth does not care what we have against it: Untruth wants us to hold it in our arms.

Scientists give so many explanations when they tell the truth, as if they were telling lies.

To be always right means defying the truth.

You cannot tell the truth in two different ways.

When you lie, God hears you. When you tell the truth, God hears and sees you.

We cannot hide what characterizes us.

The truth uttered in a law court reverberates in a different way.

How much truth do we need in order to believe it?

If we told nothing but the truth, we would speak less.

## HELP

Whenever you help, you get weaker, although on doing it you realize how strong you are.

Once you ask for help you cannot be helped.

I am glad there is nothing I could ask for help. What scares me is that there is no one I can ask to help me.

Those who ask for our help, reminding us that they helped us once, in fact claim it.

## CHOICES

In most languages "Yes" and "Ney" consists of an equal number of letters. They are the just scales of priority when we have to make a choice.

In life you have to make choices, but you don't have time to check all the options.

The servant that changes his masters boasts about his freedom of choice.

We cannot change the tumultuous history we are contemporary with, but we can choose in what direction to swim.

I have chosen to live as I was seized by desperation.

You are allowed to choose but only from my variants.

I have decided to live in reality as I know infinite can devour everything.

Even indecision is good for something. But I don't know what for.

I watch over both good and bad things but through different eyes.

Problems are missed opportunities that we did not notice on time.

Chance is a hobby given to us by God.

## MEMORIES

You can have exquisite memories of this life if you retire from it too early.

No matter how much things change, we don't buy a map, when we come back home.

Our memories are the events that make us grow old.

Any time you come back home you feel like a child again.

## SEASONS

In autumn, trees send their birds to their neighbours, then they pop into the hairdressers to get rid of extra leaves and then during the winter ball they creak as they used to, when they were young.

What winter cannot even suggest with its mountains of snow, spring can with only a few snowdrops.

Trees do not allow any of their leaves to witness winter blizzard because they want to turn green again in spring.

Spring comes more and more rarely into our life because we fall asleep in autumn, and my Lord, in vain do we snow.

Spring is vegetal cancer that got metastatic in our soul.

Winter is whiteness that seems ugly.

## WAITING

The longest wait is when there is nothing worth waiting for.

Wait is rediscovered time. Our life would come to an end sooner without expectations.

"If you do not intend to be the first to come, at least come to tell me, so I can wait for you"

Any wait irritates.

I miss what might happen to me.

I am not waiting for anybody and anything. I am not waiting for a train either.

I predict only what is not going to happen to me.

We spend half of our life thinking about the other half.

Wait is a recalculation of chances.

Wait is the invocation of time.

Wait is the patience necessary for a sacrifice.

When you are being waited for, you have to come back unexpectedly.

## MONEY

If all the people were honest, money would not have been invented.

Money is the shadow of our own body, and we have failed to get rid of it.

People take you seriously only if you pay them.

Money is the most quoted symbol.

We buy only what we cannot make ourselves.

When we buy something, we are influenced by what the ware looks like not by its price.

As long as our fortune is expressed in money, we cannot be generous.

Money is the last thing you need when you really need something.

If you want to buy something for me, don't take me to a shop! The items have already been bought by those who sell them.

Don't buy with money what you must get by yourself!

I want to be rewarded not paid.

We calculate our losses comparing them with the other people's gains.

If crafts and trades were not remunerated differentially, people could follow their true callings.

All of us value love. Most of us do it in cash.

Betting is a financial evaluation of one's personal option.

If you bet, you guarantee hope with money.

Money compromises everything we buy.

## SENIORITY

How sad that we grow old when we are at the peak of our maturity!

You are old when fashionable clothes do not suit you anymore.

When your age is no longer an advantage to you, it acknowledges what you have been going through.

I am older than Labis, Essenin and Jesus. Oh, my Lord, how fast people get old.

Quite often we wrongly believe that some people have gradually gone senile. Actually, we have grown wiser than them.

Elderly women hide their age for fear they might be thought senile.

Everything we climbed up during our youth must be climbed down during our old age. While doing it we are saying, "Oh, God, how foolish of us to have climbed so high! You feel dizzy simply by climbing down."

One's age is the shame of the un-happenings expressed in years.

While growing old our eyesight gets weaker and the loss of beauty is only partially perceived.

Only unsatisfied people hide their age.

# CHURCH

Churches are raised transversally the way to hell.

Church is the place where we meet to think about death together, after every one of us has reflected in his/her own house and realized he/she would be lost without belonging to a species.

Although religious ceremonies last long, Liturgies have not become obsolete.

Historically, men in church have been privileged above women and are anointed before them —reversing the order in which they committed the original sin. In secular life, women tend to be privileged above men and men thus sin every day in order to restore their historic position of privilege.

Although Jesus appeared on the big screen, we still hope to find Him in church.

Religions are the racism of the church.

Doctrine is a political dogma.

Our saint's name is the patron saint of our internal church.

We enter a temple, but we never ask whether it is the very one pulled down by Jesus.

## WEALTH/POVERTY

The poor are always concerned about their future, the rich analyse their past.

If a beggar does not give away to another beggar a little of what he/she has received, he/she does not exaggerate his/her helplessness.

Hungry people are less polite.

People on leading position avoid mixing with ordinary people they so much have struggled to separate from.

The rich man opens his door to a poor man only on the day he knows the latter comes with the land rent.

The rich think they will be rich in the After Life as well and thus they do not give up on their assets till the very end.

Trees do not like the rich fruit-bearing years because their branches break.

It is a shame to be rich when you are at the age when they expect you to starve.

## JOY

We should be pleased with an incomplete achievement. If it fails, we will not regret having rejoiced for nothing, but if we complete it, we will enjoy a second celebration.

Joy is stimulated happiness.

When you feel depressed, you have the feeling that things you have never wanted before might bring you satisfaction.

Celebrate your emotions with the people you associate them with.

The real satisfactions are those we imagine.

## KINDNESS

God has given us strength not because he wanted us to be more powerful, but kinder.

I am not as good as I seem, but I am not as good as I would like to be either.

Kindness is the effemination of sacrifice.

World's wellbeing is narrower than the distance between two people.

I am kind–hearted and bad-bodied. There is nothing else more angelic.

## QUALITIES

Any quality has to be accentuated by another one.

Anything that characterizes us, sooner or later, will work against us.

Don't give up on qualities we used to have. Their absence might be perceived as a flaw and their actual existence as accidental.

Talent is the ability to do something else than what you have been trained for. If you do something to perfection for a long time, you can call it routine. An eagle that catches a hare soaring with it, is talented.

## FALL

We walk about so absent-mindedly as if a possible falling were all the same to us.

If you fall several times, you can get some scars in the fortune- line of your palm.

A fall is a tucked front somersault.

## BOOKS

Books are scattered leaves from the tree of knowledge late in autumn.

If you want to be contemporary with several periods of time simultaneously, you should read.

The books you have not read take revenge.

You progress if you buy books.

I read a lot to know what has been written and to avoid repeating the world literature.

I like people in general and book readers in particular.

I read so assiduously, that the people around me think I am preparing for something.

Some people give me books and cover the price in black ink as if I were interested in their price not in their titles.

I know people by the books they keep in their bookcase. I know them best by the books they refuse to lend.

At a certain age to borrow a valuable book from someone is a shame. It is as if you borrowed the Bible.

Books are planting stock.

Books are like money. They must change hands.

A real good book makes you give up keeping a diary.

If a book is good, you can start its reading at any page.

The only means a man succeeds in fighting mortality is books.

I would like my name to outlive me mostly on a book, not on the cross.

When you don't dream at night, turn on the light and read something. Do it in compensation or as a model!

I suggest that best literary passages be included in the Bible.

The naïve guy in me has bought a book.

A house without a bookcase does not need electricity.

## MARRIAGE

Marriage means disloyalty to one's parents.

A lad proposes if he is pressed by a lass.

The man who wants to make love in the morning did not dream of his wife.

They issue two marriage certificates, one for each, and it compromises love from the very beginning.

Marriage is love besotted with papers.

Each pretense of a couple means one child minus.

The more a couple wants a child the more imperfect they become.

A man only proposes, he does not accept a proposal.

Marriage is like a compass: it always points to the north, but it is aware there are some other cardinal points.

I married for love at an early age. Thus, half of my plans came true prematurely compensating the other half that was a bit late.

How many men propose like this: "Do you want to love each other our whole life?"

A man who loves his wife the most, is the one who throughout his life, thinks about God more than he thinks about her.

A woman watches the outskirts of love -that is how far the man can see. Children run along the circumference colliding with all the men that the radius has tangentially linked, denying any secant intersection that might have stopped the peaceful rotation of the first unit.

Wedding rings are the golden handcuffs that apparently any love accepts happily.

Your wife is the comma between you and all the other women.

A wedding ring is a golden scar.

A wedding ring is the tiara, given away by the angel of love on condition we become divine in two.

## CELEBRITY

Unfortunately, fame comes only as a dessert, when you are almost fed up with any good thing that might happen to you.

Notoriety is the commercial side of glory.

I am famous. People stop me in the street. They ask me the time.

A pen name is more famous than the real name.

Don't build a too high pedestal for me. I know, that sooner or later, you will push me off.

I might be saved by glory.

By chasing perfection, glory accentuates only one thing.

Glory postpones your oblivion.

The first step to glory is when you are taken seriously.

Glory is the only consolation in front of death.

Glory is the hustle and bustle of success.

It is easy to be famous, but people acknowledge our fame with difficulty.

## **CHILDHOOD**

Einstein's brain has been studied more assiduously than his childhood.

Childhood is the happiness of being alive unawares. Sublime declines its identity.

Childhood is the foundation of life. If it quakes, life is an earthquake.

It took me so many years to grow up and now I am pining after my childhood.

Childhood is the hope that life can be different.

## NIGHTMARE

It gives me creeps thinking there are so many nightmares that fail to wake us up.

Nightmares are populated by dream characters.

The basis of a nightmare is influenced by how we get our happiness.

In the end, a nightmare seems to be the closest- to- reality dream.

## CREATION

If the world was created out of chaos, we wonder where all this perfection comes from.

A creator is always superior to his/her creation.

Now that Darwin is with God, what is telling God about the Origin of Species?

God created man on the last day of Genesis that is, on a half-day.

Anything created by God can turn into love.

God did not want to create Death, but since He was not quite successful creating Life, He should recreate it.

God loves this world dearly. He could make a better one anytime, but He doesn't.

"My Lord, each day, you recreate the world through light and leave the rest of creation to us."

If God's working day had been only eight hours long, Genesis would not have happened in a week.

God sent His created beings down on to earth for if He hadn't, they would have pushed each other into nothingness.

God would not have wanted to be recognized in His creation, but at its end, running out of inspiration, He copied his genius.

God created the world, or else His very existence would have been questioned.

Even God chose to flood the earth instead of repairing what He had created.

God noticing that his creation lasts, fears to create something else.

I hope God was pragmatic during the act of creation. I mean He has kept a look to the main chance. His main chance could not have been anything else but the divine that resides in us.

God created the world although He could have created anything else. In it we can see His divine benevolence.

# FAITH

Noticing I was alone, God called me to keep Him company.

Faith is to climb up Jacob's angelic ladder without seeing it.

"Lord, say we are right even when we are wrong, and we will continue believing in your existence."

Every day we find time to cross ourselves.

Each one of us is a John the Baptizer preparing the world for a Jesus who is holier than us.

God must think I am right if I am alive.

I have been running away from God since always, but He has been showing me the direction.

God, more than us, relies on our faith.

Optimism is pessimism looking up to God.

I breathe not to live but to sniff the sky.

If you want to admire a sunrise you don't need a map.

The sky is the only freedom I do not repress.

I look at the sky with my mortal eyes and therefore it seems so high.

If you keep the Holy Lent does not mean you love God more.

Religion is the Blue Sky. The atheists gather together when the sky is cloudy: "Look up there! We knew it."

Somebody had to understand me, and God had me in mind.

The distance between God and man is infinitely smaller than the distance between man and God. The non-believers cannot cover it, although they are not farther away from God than the believers.

We are a shadow lit by God.

In religion, one should believe not hope.

Undying love is religion.

People gave up on wanting to see God in order to understand Him.

We are in God's own image and any attempt to glamorize it, is a blasphemy.

## CROSS

My friends keep telling me: "Hey, man, you have raised your cross on a place fit for a house."

You could have incinerated me using the numerous crosses you made for me, but you were afraid I might not burn.

We all have the feeling our cross is too heavy for us to be able to rise.

## CULTURE

Culture is like water: the deeper it is the better you swim in it.

I thought I met a lot of friends in Rome, but I was told they were all statues.

The world is the representation of our idea about it.

## KNOWLEDGE

I am afraid of the unknown, but what if I knew it.

The immediate perspective of your own end gives you the real dimension of the surrounding reality.

You tell me you don't know me, then why are you calling me stranger?

'It is pitch dark within a single man' says my visually impaired ego.

I am a romantic guy in a modern world. I am going to a watchmaker to have my electronic watch battery replaced.

I don't need a mirror. I know who I am.

If we tried talking to ourselves, we would realize how poor interlocutors we are.

In spite of our respect for God, we still send reconnaissance planes into His Garden.

## COURAGE

To pluck up one's heart means to accept your superiority.

If you throw in the towel before the fight is over, next time the victory will still not be yours

When we initiate an action, we forget how old we are.

Any hero knows that his time to prove his courage is limited.

Ammunition has always stimulated the combatants' courage.

When you ask for something, you want to get it before the deadline.

We are courageous if you come up with something everybody hoped to have but they want it much later.

I don't know whether it makes sense to love each other, but certainly we have to go for it.

Unimplemented courage is pride.

## WORD

Words are the incongruities of silence.

An untold word will never defeat a written word.

We never utter the words we treasure.

Words would never have made a career if it had not been for the poets and vice versa.

The bigger the space between words is the more vigorous they become.

Words said by people who have not seen each other for a long time sound like verdicts.

Any choice of words is symbolic.

I am saying the word because silence seems false to me.

Let us not keep a tight grip on keeping our word. It is more important to get rid of it by turning it into fact.

A pedantic man gesticulates with words.

The incongruence of language makes us witty.

Words are the flowers of thought.

## DANCING

Dancing began when people, who were listening to music, could not help standing up.

Dancing is a ship of fools colliding between two soul-shaped rocks.

## GIFTS

Some people offer gifts to us because they know we preserve them better.

People who forget to lock their doors can be taken for hospitable people.

When I have run out of things to offer, you are allowed to ask me for anything you want.

When the guests arrive, we receive their gifts because we don't know what else to do with our hands.

Ask me for anything you want. It is less than I can offer.

## DIGNITY

If we are going to die one day, at least let's do it with dignity!

I am a sensitive man, I hate to be humiliated.

You can be worthy of you, and of no one else.

## SEPARATION

Departure is the saddest of all renunciations.

Any departure seems duplicitous.

Let me go by choice if you want me to miss you.

The worry about departing belongs to desperate people.

Who comes back where he/she started from, does it because he/she has got lost.

The most beautiful departures are those when you leave the real world.

When you leave, all you can see is the road.

"Adieu" is the departure curse.

When there are more friends in heaven than on earth, we have to join them.

**DESTINY**

Destiny gets the shape of the life it is poured into.

Destiny is the die in the hand of time.

Predestination is God's science fiction.

In the coffee grounds of life, death can read whether we will conquer eternity or not.

Fate is life that overtakes us.

I believe more in my destiny than in myself.

If you are waiting for your destiny, it means you can decide it.

For any man destiny starts tomorrow.

Destiny is time's jester.

Despair is the question destiny is asking us, for it wants to be sure we still accept it.

Good luck is destiny that knows how to sell its merchandise.

Corollary of Newton's Laws is: no force is stronger than destiny's force.

At the end of life, there is its destiny.

Glory is destiny's optimistic version.

I am transient but my transit is heard.

Bad things will happen, too. I'd rather be realistic than optimistic.

I stand firm in my work like a dolphin that it is going to die in the open sea.

Let's be more frightened of what might happen to us in our absence!

The greatest part of our despair is caused by the fact that we, rational beings, do not know what may happen to us.

Whatever happens to us, it is because we are present.

God is asking us to build a tower, but he is hiding its cubes.

Few people admit that their life is autobiographical.

## FORMATION

We are the most uncertain part of our future.

We are constantly evolving.

I am like a shot arrow. Who will stop me will be my goal and victory.

I die like a bunch of grapes saying: "I will be made wine anyway"

I am self-confident. I am not confident in what is going to happen to me.

Autumn crops sweeten its rains.

Thirst is the desire of the water in us to flow faster.

Any evolution surpasses its previous moods.

I don't want to start anything from the beginning. The same things keep flowing towards me, but they seem to be some children who have grown up a little.

Exercises are problems in full swing.

Progress is the preservation of values.

Anything we take seriously helps us grow up

The internal depth dictates our height.

Life set a lot of traps for me, but I released a deer from each of them.

By the time you are full-fledged, people have the feeling you are wasting your time.

Perfection shows our incapacity of going beyond our limits.

A road whose end is visible is not worth taking.

Just like a parent who sends his/her child to a vocational school, God sent me to life: "Whatever they will teach you there, it will do you a world of good when you are back".

## DIPLOMACY

Diplomacy stands for the working hours of human institutions.

Nowadays we would give Socrates the same amount of hemlock, diluted in honey.

Politeness is diplomats' curse word.

## DIVORCE

Divorce - the disclosure of wrong reasons for which two people tried to love each other.

Divorce - a heart transplant without anaesthesia.

Divorce is sometimes the only way of preserving the past unaltered.

The ex-spouses may discover new qualities in each other if they meet after the divorce.

You realize how much energy love restrains during a divorce.

If you unite two zeros you get the infinite. It certifies the theory of exhaustion through separation.

I would move divorce from the Civil Code into the Criminal Code because it is an aforethought murder of two lives, a wiping up with a wire sponge of an autobiographical fragment, regarded as ill-timed.

After a divorce you begin admiring death, because death does not ask for papers.

## LONGING

Longing is the bashfulness of coming back.

When we miss someone, it is a shame we hesitate to go all the way to love.

I miss you all, who have time to show me only love.

You can't pine for someone whose name you don't know.

When we recall a feeling, we say we miss something or someone.

## WISHES

A goldfish could grant me three wishes simply by being present: Firstly it is a fish, secondly it is a gold fish and thirdly and most important I can talk to it.

I wish I had Jesus' capacity and told the thief next to me: "Tomorrow you will be with me in paradise."

I have so many ideas, that I sometimes wish I were a retard.

One has to wish for such divine things, that simply by thinking of them, one should be pleased.

Wishes are repressed desires.

## LOVE

If you keep on postponing falling in love, when you finally accept it, it will tell you that actually it has not been looking for you.

As for me, I am not in love, but when we two are together I change my mind.

"Honey, I am a globetrotter of your feelings".

Love is the only feeling that cannot be declared on time, it has to wait.

The real love is a barefooted girl who keeps asking you to take her in your arms and carry her across the field of bloomed briars.

You cannot demand a woman to love you, but you can simply love her.

Love is the light slipped between two souls by God.

In love opinions turn into feelings.

The hard-working man's principle-what is done does not have to be done again- when applied to true love is not true.

I pity the soul that has learnt how to listen. It means it has fallen in love.

Love is like a spider web. It tears you apart when the capture is large.

When you fall in love again you change only the person, but not the feelings.

We are so fascinated by love that we forget to ask it what it has taken away from us in exchange.

Love is the sorrow that hates being alone.

If you follow her/him and she/he follows you, it means you are moving in the circle of love.

In love we know only the people in love the rest has to be created.

Love is the prerequisite of a gullible man/woman.

We know how to love, but we don't know who to love.

Love is the prayer that was listened.

There are more loves than pairs.

There are several ways of loving, but none of preserving it.

If we exclude love, life does not need action anymore.

I don't know whether it is worth loving each other but we certainly must try.

Love is a reciprocal theft with shared sentence.

Love is the sorrow whose beginning is pleasant.

Love was created in order to demonstrate that if one is alone, they can offer nothing.

In a great love story, one of the partners is unreal.

Love can be founded on interdictions only if both sides agree on them.

An aimless love cannot have rivals.

Lovers, who do not kill themselves with the same dagger, lead separate lives.

You love only whom you think will not betray you.

Othello got upset with Desdemona because by losing the handkerchief she has separated herself from all the tears of sorrow and joy that she had shed in it.

To love means not knowing this word.

The joy of loving is suppressed by the jealousy of being loved by someone else who is not you.

Although Orpheus did not succeed in his attempt of saving Eurydice, the term orphism, as metempsychosis, is still used.

When you think how little love needs, you are amazed how many people give up on it.

Great loves are not born at night.

The robot that was taught how to love, when unplugged cried.

You can really love when you have known yourself.

That part of us that does not love us, is in love with someone else.

Love is a form of death that no cemetery can hold.

In love, when you come back, actually you move ahead.

It is a big mistake to love only in the first person. Love on other people's behalf!

There is no love that does not start well.

Any love, except self-love, is holy.

When you don't say how much you love, it does not mean you love in secret, it means you love passionately.

In love we offer only that part of us which is dear to us.

There are two categories of men. Those, who first love women and then God-these men are looking for an explanation for their inconsistency, in the sky. And there are those, who first love God, and then women-these men have not understood their love of God at all.

Love is the shortest path to death.

If you want to love, first wait to be loved.

That part of you that does not love you, will never admit to it.

"Honey, you are beckoning to me. Now I realize that a cross can be a sign, too."

Love is our form of regret when we have to face the implacable law of dying alone.

"Honey, don't ask me whether my love declarations are sincere, my entire imagination suits you."

I am intrigued to find out that priests accept to deliver a marriage service only after they look over the legal document issued by a town hall. Preaching in the desert, that used to be the cornerstone of religion, no longer resonates with the noblest of certitudes, that is love.

In love we do not lie to each other. We are wrong unwillingly.

We are defined by everything we love. Everything we hate diminishes our existence.

We love everything that can be taken away.

Love is everything God has given us, apart from our body.

Love is the mirage of promises. If they are not forgotten, they lead to separation.

Love is how man can conquer the universe.

Love is the injustice we do not dare to commit to ourselves.

True loves never reveal their purpose.

Only love can dethrone you in the fortress that lies inside you.

We are the only cover between what we love and what we enweave.

One love can be betrayed only by another love, and this is not a capital sin.

By loving with our soul, we risk losing that love, but not our soul.

Love is the truth watched over by heart so as to make it come true.

Only love knows how to die. Everything else goes on living uselessly.

We have the perspective of angels when we are in love.

Love is everything you did not know before you fell in love.

People in love are some geographers. They set off bearing in mind the illusion of reaching that happiness lying in the horizon line and end up being certain the earth is round.

If we want to love, all we have to do, is to live.

Love is like committing suicide. You give up on you, thinking that you will find peace in the other world.

I love desperately because I know, I no longer belong to myself, I have totally offered myself to the woman I love and she can do whatever she wants with me.

Love asks itself the most perishable questions.

Of all forms of love the falsest ones seem to be those that do not concern us.

We should always love each other, as we would have done if we were younger.

Love is the only part of happiness it can embody to perfection.

As love checks on our faithfulness, it can ask impossible things from us.

Love compromises all our other feelings.

You don't need courage to love, you simply need someone.

Love does not change us too much, but it does it to such an extent that we become unrecognizable.

Love is powerful because it can embody a life in a second.

A girl who loves you does not even realize when you kiss her.

Love consists of two parties therefore, it can be severed anytime.

To love yourself means knowing your own limits.

We love by permanently contradicting our egotism. It explains why it is brief but noble.

Love is a circle, in which the man is the centre giving it depth, and the woman is the radius giving it amplitude.

Love needs both partners' beautiful memories to fill its uninspiring moments.

We have to admit that love needs flowers only to redecorate its Lost Paradise.

Love needs real, and not background performers.

Any love that does not denigrate itself through its own actions, is jejune.

If you love me, love me till the end!

As it happens with all the other betrayals, love starts by unbosoming itself to somebody.

Palpitations are the extra-systoles of love.

## JUSTICE

Justice is Truth's ambition.

Justice is the truth told while standing.

Prosecutors speak better than priests with the deceased.

We are right only about things that do not match.

No act of justice can justify its cruelty.

You cannot be right without giving evidence.

How unjust it is to make justice!

When you are right about yourself, it is good to know you are the last to find it out.

Justice is looking more and more like a comma.

Justice is coming to ask for the latest news.

The fighting rightness is justice.

We should not take the law into our own hands. Our justice should come from the others.

Justice is the only enduring love.

Justice is to give up on your pride to ethics' favour.

## **JOURNEY**

Journey is the delusion of distance.

Journey is the meaning given to earth with our strides.

Journeys are the paths no longer walked but run through.

But for the roads, we would not feel the need of buying cars.

Walking is the burden of the body set in motion.

After walking a lot, even driving makes you feel tired.

When we are late at the start, it does not matter where we are heading for.

I set off on a journey not because I know it, but because I like it.

To start again from the beginning does not mean you decline your experience.

If someone is asking you where you are coming from, they obviously are not interested in where you are heading for.

If you decide to start a journey you should stop counting the stones on the road.

Ask someone to follow you and they are going to ask you whether you are going their way.

The beginning cannot last, but it can be continued.

Every time we come back home, we realize that our departure has been a mistake.

If I come back on the same path, it means I have been defeated.

It is useless taking a path whose end is in sight.

Life is a race. It does not matter how many people you have overtaken, what matters is how many laps you have run.

Unfortunately, your legs not your mind decide the direction of your journey.

Any road ahead is a road no one has travelled on before.

Any road on which we can travel back is safe.

Each step we take can be risky because it influences our foothold.

My body is Magellan's sailing ship sailing around the world and does not want any credit for it. It just wants to prove that the earth is round.

God is showing us the way and we are asking Him where it leads to.

Even if I do not reach the sky, I have the chance of dying on my way to it.

I can take only one human with me on the path to heaven–he/she must know the way very well, because somewhere there is a fork in the road, and next we will see each other again up in heaven.

I am in such a hurry that I could travel at night, too.

I always come back where I started from – I like to be taken for a beginner.

The most beautiful journeys are those done in twos.

May each journey be to your advantage and may each advantage contribute to your development!

Any farewell wish heard when you leave is food for thought.

We can find out where a human is heading to, by asking them where they are coming from.

If you want to check how you managed to reach the summit you have to climb down.

When my shadow is projected in front of me, I am asking myself what direction I should be going.

As long as God is up, we still have to climb up.

## GOD

People who doubt God's existence because they have not seen Him, should consider themselves extinct, for their soul has not shown itself either.

God is what is left after we have been thinking about Him.

You cannot see God if you do not have a ladder, that can take you up to heaven.

Jesus' sacrifice proves that those who are not understood on earth will be understood in Heaven. Jesus was so much hurt while living among humans that when he came to life again, He showed Himself only to those who believed in Him. He didn't put up any longer with the enemies of His own prophesies He could have produced the piece of evidence that they had come true, but He did not do it. Thus, Jesus stays in the faith sphere of the soul looking up to heaven avoiding the rigorous Cartesian demonstration. Experiences are Biblical but their agglutinations change them into science.

All the meetings in our life precede the meeting with God.

God would rather reveal Himself outside than inside the church.

God is in heaven not to be away from us, but to wait for us up there.

God's solitude is Heaven's plenitude.

God does not look at our life as if it were a thriller. He steps in for us irrespective of how exciting the plot might be.

As people want to understand God, they have given up on their desire to see Him.

The idea of God is connected with the idea of Heaven. We cannot see it around us but if we rise high enough, heaven can become very visible here on earth.

God is kind. In His kindness He is alone, though.

God walks on churches like a yogi does on needles. He does not crush them, they do not make Him bleed and we, believers, feel protected.

If God had not conceived, woman would have failed the Creation.

We are playing hide and seek with God. From the very beginning we are told where we may hide. "Can I hide in heaven?", I ask pinpointing a cloud. "No, I am hiding there" God answers. And the game begins.

If God came down on earth, He would avoid people.

God measures eternity in people.

What is extraordinary is that we say God's name even when we swear.

The world could have been more stable if man had not realized he was made in God's own image.

God does not show Himself to all humans at the same time, but to only one at a time every day.

God does not call our names. He also looks at us.

People that are afraid of God when it thunders, do not glorify Him when the sun shines.

Love is the religion God is going to be born in.

Jesus is the supreme sinner, who has taken upon Him the sins of the world. We shall be redeemed when we take upon us the evils we have not committed.

When you address angels, God hears you.

To ask God to show Oneself, is like asking Jesus to die again.

Pontius Pilate's words, "Ecce Homo", represent both Jesus' supreme crowning as human and the negation of His divine origin.

When gods greet us, the sun rises.

God is the director who does not allow us to be extras.

God is the kindness that does not show its identity.

We think about God far less than He does about us.

## FOES

We always make new friends although foes are always more interesting.

If you don't fight with your foe when they want, they get very upset.

If my enemies were as unhappy as I am, I could easily defeat them.

There are two kinds of enemies: those who declare war on you and those who say that if they had been by you, they would have supported you.

Our enemies would like us to stay with our mistakes.

A moment of sincerity to your enemy could be fatal to you.

I admire my enemies because they know who to fight with.

When our enemies praise us, we can be certain our victory is to their advantage.

Foes that amplify our mistakes are afraid of us.

Enemies ask us questions without waiting for our answers.

Our enemies find fault with everything that makes us their superior.

It is a cruel thing to constantly defeat the same enemy.

Christian -love -your -enemy doctrine turns the external war into an internal one. It is about fighting against your own vanities.

We should behave with our enemies as light behaves with darkness. We win because our enemies are offered the opportunity of ruling at the same time with us.

The most dangerous way of getting rid of your enemies is, to make them your friends.

I criticize my enemies calling them on their first names to avoid being too severe.

If we knew our enemy was pursuing us, we would eat up even the peels of the oranges.

Who did not call you back, loathed you.

As long as my foes fight to decide which one of them to attack me, I stay calm.

## **HEROES**

In history heroes are suicidal.

I am the hero who has got old, waiting for his turn to sacrifice himself.

We could have become generals in the length of time required to become heroes.

You choose the pedestal after you have finished the statue.

Only those who have had a hard life, have the chance of becoming heroes after death.

## ESSENCE

The essence of a thing lies outside it.

Essence is less than structure, but we value it more.

We implore fate to tell us what the essence of life is, and it answers with some heroic deeds out of which we are not able to select the essential.

The big issues of the world are in fact man's necessities.

Essence is the stable stock.

We would cease looking at ourselves in the mirror if we were not after our personality's reflection.

## EGO/I

It is we who are in our own universe.

Mirror is the only self-portrait worth being framed.

I am what you would have been if you had been in my shoes.

God is testing His ambitions in me.

Whatever happens to me, can happen to anyone. I am universal.

We are the first part of a world that we are setting up.

"Lord, when you see me why do I remind you of Adam?"

Whenever I drew my self-portrait I used so much colour that all my acquaintances told me "This is Alexander the Great", "He is Napoleon", "This is Ivan the Terrible". I gave up using colours, I wiped my face and all of them said in one voice "Jesus Christ, Veronica's handkerchief has flooded you with tears."

### ACTION/DEED

Motivation is everything action expects from us.

The bad experiences of our life can be retrieved in our good deeds.

Our problems lie in their consequences.

Motivations sense actions.

You cannot praise anyone more than their own actions can.

## WOMAN

The ideal woman is the creative Eve with a sense of sin well-printed in her head.

A woman is beauty defined in space.

Women spend most of their life in front of the mirror, while men spend most of their life in front of women.

Trivia are charming only when uttered by a woman in love.

A miracle is an immaterial woman.

If you can convince a woman to stop crying, then you can convince her to let you kiss her.

Woman is the only philosopher that does not have to say a single word.

Women who know love's secret but do not use it, are in love.

Women that regret, actually regret they have nothing to regret.

A woman who is not beautiful is like a petty trader who sells her wares dear.

Women have not learnt how to love because men do not feel like teaching them.

When you go on a holiday together with a woman you must rest well before.

Women think only about love although they do not seem to.

A woman who dies before her man, wishes for it.

How impolite women are! They take off their clothes when they are kissed more passionately.

When a woman complains about not being kissed enough, she wants to be kissed more often, not just at night.

Beautiful women wear broad-brimmed hats in order to shade off their breasts.

I like women who do not realize how beautiful they are.

A woman is closer to God than man is, due to her gift of giving birth.

All women are Saints Mary. First, they conceive their baby in their mind with the Holy Ghost.

God offered the woman to man so he was not alone, but He did not suspect she would make him children.

No woman has really understood me. They couldn't wait to love me.

A beautiful woman deceives with her whole body.

Some women are so curious, that they would like to be buried with their head above the grave so as to be able to see who will die next.

From the height of her breasts any woman thinks she can dominate a man.

Women would not feel flattered if men did not tell a few white lies when they declare their love to them.

A beautiful woman and her shadow have something in common: they both lay their heart at your feet if you know how to look at them.

Breasts are the icicles of heart's great ice age.

The inauguration of a woman starts with her lubrication, then she is caressed and in the end the Sabine woman in her is raped.

Any woman has more expectations from fecundity than from her husband.

Like Saint Francis I make women of snow and then I ask them whether they are cold.

If women got pregnant just by kissing men, men would be more spiritual with them.

If a woman makes a mistake this is a bit sensual, if a man makes a mistake this is a bit stupid.

Breasts are still the most sensual way of storing milk.

## HAPPINESS

Happiness means getting used to hardships, to a reality that suits us.

Happiness means giving up on certitudes.

Happiness is amnesia of failures.

"Come happiness, but don't ask me why I am calling you so late!"

If you make me happy, I will owe you one. I don't like being indebted to anyone.

Happiness can be started again from the beginning but with different sufferings.

Come happiness! My internal despair wants to meet you.

No matter how well happiness knows us, it never calls us on our first names.

A sceptic never answers when Happiness calls him/her. He/she thinks it calls him/her out of despair.

Whatever we win in life, is in fact the restoration of some of our lost happiness.

People who do not understand happiness think you are mad. Those who do, think you are lucky.

Happiness never comes uninvited.

Happiness is a window that opens only from inside.

The happiness we remember with sadness has not fulfilled its goal.

The happiness you learn, you can teach, but you cannot apply.

Nothing can lead us to despair better than a previous happiness.

"My love, I can give you anything, but if you do not tell me what you really want, I cannot make you happy."

Happiness is the possible despair.

Unhappiness is the transition stage between Good and Evil. When Evil has come, you can no longer be unhappy, you have to fight.

An optimist knows that any happiness can be the last one. A pessimist is sure of it.

Happiness belongs to those who can apprehend it.

People should not set off in the pursuit of happiness in compact groups.

We are too impatient to be happy, that we do not prepare well for it.

Misfortunes that come to an end are genuine lies.

Come Happiness! Do not ask me why I have called you!

No happiness can impose itself in front of misfortunes that explain it.

It is sad that happiness depends more on what we have not done than on what we have done.

Lasting happiness is, in fact, postponed happiness.

By getting your happiness shipshape, it will disintegrate.

Happiness is served hot, in cracked bowls.

Happiness represents an individual's capacity of adapting his/her dream to reality.

The most durable happy moments are those we forget about, storing them somewhere in our mind.

Efforts made to achieve happiness take longer than happiness.

Happiness is measured in moments and thus it fails when it has to face sadness.

When we have everything, we need to be happy, we realize people have lost their patience and stopped watching us.

You can write about your happiness only if you wait for it.

I am an expert in statistics. I have accounted for my happiness, and I filled half a page.

When you start boasting, people realize you are unhappy, because you have no one to reveal your achievements to.

Imagine you are happy. If your sleeves are plucked, you must know it is not happiness that is doing it.

If you are not happy while young, you will never be.

We shouldn't love each other in those moments when we are happy.

When we are happy, we realize there are too many useless friends around us, whom we are supposed to confess our state of mind. Just like some worn-out condensers they do not charge, and they start embarrassing our beatitude.

Happiness turns the sandglass of life upside down.

Happiness is like getting used to hardships, to a reality that suits us.

Happiness is like giving up on certainties.

Justice is for the crowd. Freedom is for a few. Happiness is for nobody.

Alas, you, happy people! You have so many happy moments that you have no time left to laugh.

If we are contented with what we have, it does not mean we are happy.

# PHILOSOPHY

People used to go into a public place to listen to Socrates. Now they go there to buy green groceries.

Philosophy is the elixir of mandrake.

A philosopher is a man who says he would buy a horse but only if he found a horseshoe. When he finally finds the horseshoe, he concludes: "Now I have a horseshoe but I still cannot find my horse. I have only burdened myself."

Socrates' death is the death of philosophy.

Philosophy is what God would have told us about life.

If I did everything I say, I would lose the fame of being a philosopher.

A philosopher cannot be loved for his thoughts, but he can be forgiven for them.

When the philosophers left, they said it was up to me to switch the light off. I didn't switch it off and you continue teasing each other as if nobody could see you.

When the Greeks were talking to the gods, they were actually talking to themselves.

To philosophize is to let your thoughts out of your mind.

I think so fast that I forget what I have to do.

I don't do too many things, but you could employ me to babysit your ideas.

## PHYSISCS

A force that has only acceleration, but no mass, gets away from the destination.

If I loved all the people at the same time, I would kill myself. I would be useless. I would annul the Brownian motion.

I wonder whether gravitational acceleration for birds is 9.834 m/s 2.as well.

The different time zones help half of the world to repose and prevent the whole earth from exploding.

Einstein's theory of relativity demonstrates that not even science relies on certitudes Relativism, through its broad spectrum, governs the world.

When we die, we purify by depositing and when we pray we purify by evaporating.

The speed towards victory is measured in time unit.

## FEAR

Fear is sadness placed in the future.

Courage is fear's vanity.

Your enemies' shadows are scarier than your enemies are.

Even when one is fed up with living, one is still afraid of death.

Fear of Death is the externalization of passion for our internal beauty.

I am afraid of you, not of your power.

Witness always narrates from the perspective of the party that could not intervene.

I have the courage to say I am afraid.

When we set off hesitatingly even the road is getting narrower.

Fear is that part inside us that has got mature too early.

Cowards arrogate everything to themselves.

A rabbit knows it is scared of its own shadow, all the more so because it magnifies its proportion.

I am afraid that in heaven we might meet those people we stopped meeting on earth.

We pull down a construction, for fear we might be held responsible for its failure to last long.

I am so powerful that I am scared of myself.

Only people who know their names will be forgotten when they die, are afraid of death.

We live in a world we are afraid to populate.

We want to go to heaven, but we are afraid to live higher than the fifth floor.

In man's world it is beauty and among mushrooms it is the bright colours that signal danger.

## THOUGHTS

A thought is the parsimony of thinking.

A thought is rather cheeky than wise because it dares to leave us.

Thoughts are soul's crutches.

I don't read. I only compare my thoughts with what the others have written.

Just like children who babble in order to learn how to speak, we think amorphously in order to materialize ideas.

If a thought did not fly, it would be a human.

When I think well, I sleep rough at night.

To meditate means to get angry because you are having a very fast thought.

My thoughts have not been polite with me.

I used to have a thought. I don't know who has taken it away from me. Who can give it back to me?

A thought that does not turn into action, fails.

We deserve the shame that does not give us food for thought.

The thoughts that come true without our help are premonitions.

We are in a pensive mood not because of our thoughts but of our worries.

If the apricot blossom did not open, its fruit would be bitter. Any thought we keep to ourselves becomes malefic.

"Mens sana in corpore sano" This is the old Latin adage about the thought that takes the shape of the body in which it is born.

The limit of a thought is the word, not the action.

An obsession is the boomerang of the thought. The farther you want to throw it, the harder it hits you.

Our most optimistic thoughts can be placed among hopes therefore, they can hardly come true.

Both what we say and what we think matter equally.

Thinking is like a billiards ball which is null if it doesn't touch another ball.

"Oh, my thought, give me some of your power!"

The thoughts that do not simplify our life, perpetuate it. Children do not simplify our existence.

A good thought is the thought we feel guilty for not having had it, from the very beginning.

A good thought should be followed by a similar deed.

Our deeds refresh our thoughts.

A lot of thoughts did not make the grade, trying to turn into actions.

If I cannot utter a thought, I write it down.

The last thought should be the thought of dying.

I good thought without action is like a beautiful woman who is lying to you.

A man is superior to oneself through one's thought.

A thought upsets our soul more than pain.

May we think at least as convincingly as we speak!

I am looking for a William Tell to shoot the apple of my thought off my head.

If only forget-me-nots bloomed on my grave, you would still have to think twice

An idea is the thought one and only.

My fearful thoughts are hidden deep inside, and I can tempt them out only with paper, ink, and a handful of love.

An idea is the illusion lost by an angel.

Fixed ideas are the crystals of the mind.

Nights are suitable for sleeping. If during the night you wake up and can't help thinking, then imagine that days are suitable for sleeping and start from the beginning.

If you are impressed more by my thought, at least ask it how much I have insisted on it meeting you.

Ideas keep the rhythm of a novel.

One's own vision is called creation.

## JEALOUSY

The same as light combined with darkness harms the eyes more than pitch dark can, jealousy, a combination of love and hatred, is infinitely bitterer and crueller than hatred itself.

Jealousy without adultery is stimulating.

In love any lie is believed, while in hatred, any truth condemns.

Jealousy is nurtured with overabundant love.

## GENIUS

Something interesting continues to happen to geniuses even after their death.

There are three stages in dealing with a genius. He/she is negated, then he/she is accused of plagiarism, and finally he/she is acknowledged. Each stage can last for more than two hundred years.

Glory is the memorial service held to memorialize a genius.

## MISTAKE/FAULT

If people forgive us, God can forgive us sooner.

Nature fury supplies us with an excuse for our temper tantrums.

Any excuse is an abuse of trust.

## IDEAL

An ideal is the pragmatism of soul.

Once an ideal is achieved, the temple, where you have prayed your entire life, seems covered with ivy.

An ideal is today's dream.

## ILLUSION

A mirage can tempt only someone who walks in a desert.

People who strongly want something can get it broken.

The wind stirs the dust to prevent us from seeing how the rain is born.

The sunrise announces very little sunshine.

In my illusions I am the only one who takes oneself seriously.

If we are victorious only because we are alive, then the race is somehow loaded.

A lot of flowers bloom only to tempt the bees.

## INDIFFERENCE

I love you with the indifference with which you hate me.

Sincere indifference is foolish.

Indifference cannot make us famous.

Contemplation is the ardour of indifferent people.

# INTELLIGENCE

An optimist can rely on his/her intelligence as long as he/she does not hesitate.

At any age we are sure that nature cannot change us more than it has already done.

After a storm we are so impressed by the clear blue sky that we no longer pay attention to the puddles.

If something good happens to us too soon, it does not impress us.

We think that some people are intelligent because they do not tell us who they quote.

If you outspeak other people, they will tell you to keep quiet.

If something absurd is commented, it loses its mystery.

A benchmark should be the starting point and not the point of arrival.

We would rather regret what has happened to us than why it has not happened to us.

Depending on how we die, we become immortal or not.

When you are offered something, it covers only the first part of the blackmail.

I know so many things because I am fond of them, not because I am intelligent.

## HYPOCRISY

The moon has two faces. A man has one thousand faces.

I am not going to take my role seriously as long as I play it well.

Palm is the favourite part of a fist. It can both caress and strike.

## TEMPTATION

I am swimming to you, my darling, ignoring the sirens who keep telling me I could become a famous swimmer.

A hooker is perfect if one is satisfied just by thinking about her.

Any condom automatically stirs the desire to have sex.

## HISTORY

History is the life of mankind seen through the eyes of several heroes.

History is the contortion of time.

History teaches us that any peace is a truce.

You'd better owe to life than to history.

## TRUST

If you don't trust people, you fool yourself. If you trust people, they will betray you.

Trust is the way you believe something is more important than what you believe.

Trust is permanent hope.

I have more confidence in a soldier during a battle than in a general after a battle.

## URGES

Let's not forget we are the angels of the same Sky!

Let's not complain about today, let's complain about the life we have lived so far!

Let's not give our life the opportunity to miss us, because any departure is a checkout of a possible betrayal!

Let's act in solidarity! A beehive consists of all its bees, and they do not gather honey from only one flower.

If you are not capable of doing anything good in your life, at least do some bad things so as to be given as a negative example.

If you are interested in something you must get it, not wait for it.

Advice is like stars. Following a star you do not pay attention where you are going and you may fall, but if you ignore it you will never arrive at the destination.

Don't move your hands if you are not in water!

There is always someone ready to give you advice after you make a mistake.

Don't slam the door before you go out.

Stop asking me things I don't know or else you will be dissatisfied with my answers.

In your future do not ask for things you have not asked for today.

## DEFEAT

A defeat is the victory that is testing your patience.

When justice does not side with the winner, the loser has to continue the fight.

When you are defeated, you do justice to the others.

The only loser is the one who defines oneself as such.

There are no shooting stars for real as long as none of them has fallen on the ground.

Of all the stars in the sky, the shooting stars are the most watched.

I decided to ask only questions and write them down for a whole day. The nest day looking through them I realized that half of them were the answers to the others but asked the other way around.

Let's not admit ourselves defeated only after the danger has passed and its laurels have been snatched.

We admit nothing of what can compromise us, and this compromises us the most.

The antidote of defeat is not oblivion but revenge.

Someone down on his/ her knees cannot hurt you unless he /she is asking something from you.

Who mourns his/her dead on the battlefield, capitulates and by doing it, he/ she profanes their sacrifice.

## QUESTIONS

Many questions are asked only to denigrate their own answers.

An answer can never fully exhaust a question.

In an ambiguous world, questions only complicate things.

We tell our life only to those who are in such a hurry that they do not have time to ask us questions.

I have the best answers to the questions you don't ask me.

The people who know how to answer, are those who have asked themselves most of the questions.

It is better to rephrase a question than to wait for the answer.

The force of asking questions defines the potential of giving answers.

The questions are so beautiful that the answers stick like a bur to them.

A well-asked question guides itself by the answer.

If you ask a question and you answer it, it is called Socratic, but when God answers it, it is called catechism.

I wish I could forget the question the moment I find out the answer.

You are asking me how I am, and other people give you the answer.

I have the feeling I have achieved something extraordinary. There is no one I can ask. All the people around me are mediocre.

If you do not ask the question well, you complicate it.

## UNDERSTANDING

To repeat something means double understanding.

When I realized how many people died, I understood that to live is to pray for them.

When the first prize is not awarded it means God has competed as well.

We are not allowed to live when we realize it compromises us.

The uselessness of things derives from their consequences.

I understand your silence the best.

Whatever we achieve and consequently, we do not start it again, is not a genuine achievement.

Events we do not understand will happen again.

The misunderstood justice is not just.

Just by reading "The Train Timetable" you can learn something. Things like –there is a cyclicity of arrivals and departures, speeds are predestined to us and irrespective of how much you accelerate only the right direction takes you to your destination.

Some teachers want to show us both what we don't know and what they don't know.

As soon as we understand something we tend to explain it.

Whenever someone asks me to explain to them what I have written, I feel like a sculptor who is begged to carry his/her own granite statues on his/her back and take them into a fan's house.

You should never ask anybody to answer your question unless they ask you the same question.

The weaker your eyesight gets, the richer your imagination becomes. Now I can understand Homer's secret.

A fool never pretends to be smart when he/ she on his /her own.

We suffer in vain if we do not know why.

I have to say I understand or else I would understand nothing.

The dignity of living is similar to the shamelessness of understanding.

Never have I been understood by the people around me, that is why I like travelling.

Don't expect anything from me, it is all I am asking from you!

Unless we learn from our enemy, they will defeat us.

If we knew our enemies better, we would side with them.

When people turn us down, we ask fate to help us.

If you are defeated with your own weapons, it is as if you killed yourself.

If you do not ask for your rights, it means you do not know them.

Shards bring luck, but then someone has to make up for the damage.

God, forgive my enemies! They have whispered in Your ear about my broken promises.

Silence is squirming among uttered words while I am trying to understand them.

What I don't understand, I can't combat and what I understand, I have to defend.

We realize where a human is heading for if we ask them where they are coming from.

A camel would not succeed in crossing the desert without the water supply in its hump. A burden makes us resistant.

A friend is the best enemy you could have had.

There is an Absolute we cannot understand and an Absolute we do not know.

The harder you learn something, the better you understand it.

You should know that death is sympathetic to us. It does not care how we die.

The North Star has never intended to guide us to the most unfriendly icy realms, it only points to the North.

The wind helps trees bear fruits. A change brings about a novelty.

It is not only Australia that is down under. We are down under, too. It is all about whom or what we relate to.

Like a person stripped for knowledge, whatever I learn, I forget to be able to commit something else to my memory.

What you have not understood, has happened to you too fast.

In the race of ideas, the one that arrives at the finishing line first, is the weakest.

The priorities that surpass interests are ethical.

Everything I don't understand, I take seriously

By reducing everything to its essence we risk not understanding it.

When you understand everything that happens to you, it means that all things that happen to you are simple.

We love so little that hatred can do whatever it wants with us.

Everything we reproach ourselves for, will be reproached with us later.

History teaches us how to miss those people we did not meet when they were alive.

Zero is a good beginning but only in string of numbers.

Whatever happens to us in life is because we accept nothing else.

The right to immortality is more important than the right to life.

Why we get angry is so unimportant that next time we will only laugh at it.

Things that will happen to us are more important than what has happened to us.

No museum could have held any of the seven wonders of the ancient world.

The point of view from where things seem favourable must be chosen from the sphere of our interests.

The big issues are those we cannot solve ourselves.

In history if you step aside, you accept to be led by others.

It is obvious that those who say they have understood us before we finish our demonstration want to borrow our point of view.

Compared to oxygen our role in sustaining life is minor.

To dedicate oneself to an idea does not mean surrendering to it.

In time we make our peace with any death, whereas any life can become unbearable.

When you start climbing a hill you realize it is a mountain.

Any acceptance starts with acknowledging the flaws and ends up by amplifying them.

## LAST JUDGMENT

All good things will happen one day, namely on the Last Judgment Day.

I have a hunch that on the Last Judgment Day all the questions will be asked in English.

We will deny nothing at the Last Judgment.

Do not rely on witnesses at the Last Judgment for they will be judged at the same time with you!

Armageddon has been postponed for want of a competent adjudicator.

## TEARS

Crying is the commission of pain. Tears can dissolve a lot of suffering, don't forget it!

Regret is the crying that hides its tears.

A tear on their cheek can be seen only in close-up.

When I cry my gondolas collect the water.

A sweet kiss melts the tear salt.

Only by crying you can change your state of mind.

Tears are not so pure after all, they wash our soul.

I am crying to purify my soul just a little bit.

When we cry our whole soul turns into water. The heart, observing Archimedes' law, pours it over the eyelids and what is left, we close with a smirk and say: "No problem. I won't die because of it."

Tears make sorrows seem ridiculous.

## COWARDICE

We have so much saved strength that each of us is a coward of his/her latent energies.

Cowardice relies more on disbelief than on fear.

I would give up on many things if I were offered something in exchange.

If we did not accept our life to the last moment, we could die with more dignity.

We would rather have rights than be right.

I have always thought we could get rid of our shadow if we had it painted white.

A coward is the hero that overestimated himself/herself.

## GREEDINESS

With your mouth full it is impossible to eat like a well - behaved person.

There is so much sky above us, but we still think about the earth's riches.

People have a church built only if they have bricks left after they have had a house built.

## FREEDOM

Freedom is the art of dying standing.

Freedom is the flag which if it is not hoisted cannot flutter.

We allow everything we were forbidden.

Any accepted thing is an imposed thing.

Just like the sea I know my limits, but I do not like to accept them.

I breathe but I don't want to steal anybody's air.

We increase our own freedom by observing the other people's freedom.

We could do to perfection all the forbidden things.

People that are not ready to die for their freedom, love their life too much to be able to understand it.

If only God had had enough available clay, then He would have given man a lot of autonomy.

Moses broke the Tables of the Law to show that God did not want to impose Himself by them, first and foremost.

## LIGHT

Light changes its colour every hour but it stays pure.

The ceiling of the Sky rises together with the Sun.

It is the Moon we treasure, not the Sun that lights it.

The sunshine has all the colours of the rainbow. It is exactly like the variety of all those it lights.

The stars that watch over us during the night, go on doing it during the day.

The Sun is the same for all of us, only our shadows are different.

Light is the Sky full of stars.

The Sun accepts the shadow, so we can look at it without covering our eyes with our hand.

The night is the Sun's prudish attitude towards both the people in love and thieves.

God has given us the light and we have decomposed it into photons.

**FIGHT**

A truce can only add fuel to the fighting.

I have made peace with myself, but suspicion still goes on as it always happens between two ex-aggressors.

I confront my enemies with my bare hands, and they think I want to embrace them.

The difference between the Marathon Greek soldier and marathon runners is the fact that the latter have nothing to announce.

Windows prove that the roof had nothing to do with the sky.

Too many concessions can weaken peace that is fragile anyway.

No war is supposed to last for too long.

Wars started because people wanted to know the world by holding weapons in their hands.

The peace we don't want is a truce.

The only durable peace is love.

All retired generals become peacemakers.

We cannot help being impressed by victory even if we are losers.

From the One Hundred Years War one can come back but very old.

If we joined all the wars together, we will get a history much longer than the current one.

A war is endured much better than a siege.

A sport that loses its game quality, becomes a war.

Any weapon one cannot cut bread with, is more sophisticated than a knife.

We can defeat our opponents faster if we respect them.

The bullets we shoot to the sky are fleas in the angels' wings.

We grow stronger if we go on fighting.

## **MOTHER**

Jesus is an Adam who understood that mother's love is more important than tempting Eve.

When a woman gives birth, even her husband should be given milk because he also misses her breasts.

When a woman is pregnant, the government should pay two unemployment benefits.

When mothers stop breast feeding their babies, they start experiencing the separation from their baby complex.

A man rejects his girlfriend because of the primordial comparison to maternal perfection.

If our mothers had not weaned us, we would love them even now.

Of all the loves we experience on earth, the maternal one is the most platonic and consequently, the closest to God's.

## MATHEMATICS

Observing the number theory, we know that zero, the origin, can annul everything.

The infinite line is its own limit.

Zero is the negation that allows you to build.

Zero is a number that does not exist.

Only prostitutes rely on number theory.

## MEDICINE

Patients are afraid of doctors when they discover how much the latter know about so many bad things.

Some doctors are so blasé about illness stereotype that they assume that the medical advice they have given, should have been heard by all the others.

People die on their feet because they do not understand doctors' handwriting. People do not go through with their thought because the philosophers play volleyball with it.

There are drugs that kill the pain, but they don't kill the memory of it.

Doctors' guilt is not that they do not cure all the diseases, but that they don't consider all of them treatable.

## MEMORY

Memory is the time we managed to stop in us.

An amnesic that has lost his/ her identity documents can be considered a newly born.

Memory, the queen of recollections, reigns in a non - existent kingdom.

No amnesic forgets to eat.

Memory is the most sensitive witness. It tells only what has impressed it.

The real memorization does not keep all the memories, it selects them.

It is easier for us to write down our memories than to read them.

Memory is the stone oblivion.

Memory likes to look at us from a distance.

Memory is a piece of evidence that gives a meaning to the past.

**LIE**

A lie is the spokesperson of truth.

We are not forced to tell the truth, but for sure we are not allowed to lie either.

Death is a repulsive girl, but she badly wants to keep company with us.

I want to die early so as to enjoy death longer.

I don't know how to die. If I don't learn how, I will be lost.

As I pretend being alive, people avoid my tomb.

As it is sure of its power, Death allows us to live as long as we want.

Death is after very little ad infinitum.

We die when we breathe out into the wing of our soul.

Death does not like the idea of starting everything all over again.

Death, like any capital thing, has a bad start.

One of the cruellest sophisms is that those who gave you birth are responsible for your death.

We die just once, but we feel alive again infinitely.

Death should have the trumps of an ideal girlfriend i.e. she has to wait for you for a life time and when she meets you she must satisfy you immediately.

If we could live one more day after we die, we would realize how useless we were.

The star which will fall when I die, might touch the earth.

Just like the entire nature, I can delay my degradation only by dying.

I will enjoy living till the day I die.

The convict in me knows that he will be released when I die.

We fall just like the leaves do, in order to be trampled by those whose oxygen is supplied by us.

I am dying my own way, by not living well.

It seems someone has died. The street is not that crowded. People have been bunching up on the thoroughfare leading to the cemetery.

We are born without being asked and we die at request.

To live is to die a useless death.

The more intense you live, the more time you will spend with death.

To be young is a privilege, the privilege of looking at death in a detached way.

It is not fair to die, without realizing why you lived for.

The difference between the first and last moments of our life is that when we are born no one asks us whether it hurts.

Death is time's short circuit.

We are born immortal. Gradually we accept death.

When we are born, no one tells us we are going to die.

If I don't die as I want, I may live a long life.

Death is life's travesty that suits it best.

Death is to be hard up under the ground.

Death is life's gravitational force.

Cemeteries are the only fields that people till, without waiting for a harvest.

When I get in touch with the deceased ones, they invariably ask me the same questions - "Does it still rain?", "Are there still wars?", "Are women's breasts still pointed outward and their thighs curved?"- My answer to the first two questions is affirmative, but to the last one is negative lest they might be sorry for having gone.

I will die on a sunny day and my rheumatism isn't going to warn me.

## MODESTY

They do not award a prize for modesty.

Those who step aside are those who are trampled on their toes.

You are right about everything you are saying about me. The only problem is that you should be talking to me.

I wouldn't like anybody to have a wrong opinion about me before asking me.

You can get to God only if you are modest.

## WORK

No diamond shines before it is well polished.

True champions do not need prizes.

I am writing a lot since I will not live long anyway.

Work started long before salary, but it will continue without it.

The mountain you are climbing is your pedestal.

Nobody can boast for ever with the foundation he /she has built. He/ she has to have the house built.

The most transferable right is the right to work.

I am like a plant with only one employee.

## MUSIC

They have come up with a lot of explanations about Beethoven's deafness, but none of them was about the divinity of his music.

Serenades reassures the stars that the earth in inhabited during the night as well.

A tune is the composer's breathing while agonizing in his/ her desperate anxiety.

Music is the echo of light.

## MADNESS

Madness is the private exteriorization of a feeling.

Madness is life that decides to live on its own without appealing to its holder.

A mad man is someone who has understood the things nobody else is interested in.

Madness provides you with an excuse for not finding out the truth.

Death is insignificant if we take into account one's entire life madness.

Beware of mad people, no matter how much their absurdities may attract you.

My madness is so beautiful, that it would be a greater madness to give up on it.

## LUCK/ CHANCE

Luck is a word that has been invented by atheists. Our fate is decided by God.

Gambles with fabulous stakes defame themselves because of the lottery tickets sellers, who never get rich, although the supposed treasure might have been in their hands.

We think we are unlucky if our luck is taken by someone else.

You recognize a chance when it happens because it cannot be delayed.

The chances we have lost, had been in someone else's hands.

A great idea is an idea that crosses your mind in time.

Dawn opens the sun the chance of rising.

Death is our last chance to finally meet God.

Luck is the form of future that suits you.

There is no bad luck. There are only missed chances.

Waiting for our chance is as if we were in a station where it does not stop.

Bad luck is the error factor of ambition.

Chance is such a perverse woman. It can smile at you, while lying in someone else's arms.

Our missed chances were in someone else's arms

The luck line is in God's palm.

## HUMAN/MAN

God loves the world He has created and because of it He shed a tear called man.

Humans' main duty is to love their fellow people. Then they have to forget helping them and claim nothing in exchange.

A lot of people are slaves. They have dimensions but not direction.

Honest people make mistakes only when they lie.

Let's help our fellow people with the same force God keeps us in a vertical position in spite of gravitation law.

People believe only those stories they hear.

People who have hurt us are those whom we have allowed to know our weak points.

Humans do not invent, they only name.

The people who are the most honest to us are those who allow us to find the truth on our own.

Quiet people are those people who can project anything in the future.

The most powerful people are those who succeed in reducing the world to their own scale.

People that are at the same level with us, are those people who can understand our weak points.

People who cannot meet, have wanted it.

A strong man is known by his face features. A weak man is known by his hand features.

Animosities happen naturally because there are several people who live in one body.

Humans are the lightning rods of God's sorrows.

Humans are the angels of a telluric sky.

Humans are the stars smashed to the ground.

We are the angels that God has endowed with legs that are stronger than their wings.

## CONCEIT

The pride of a single man would have been enough for all the gods in Olympus.

You can be proud if you get rid of your vanity.

Haughtiness is the pride that started making victims.

A female hare is proud if it is chased by a lion.

Vanity is the power with which a king wears his crown.

People that are not after success are the winners in the fight against their own pride.

Vanity is feminine pride.

Pride always finds radical solutions.

Actually, it is the pride that is awarded a prize.

If you are proud, you are your own enemy.

If I thanked you, you would think I owe you.

## PARADOXES

The paradox of love is the following: to love each other we must know each other, but the better we know each other the less we love each other.

The paradox of lies is: the more beautiful they are the less they want to be in truth's company.

What a paradox! What characterizes us must be expressed and become our appearance.

The paradox of creation is to create a human who asks you why you have created him/ her.

I am bowing in front of the beauties of the world- both material and imaginary-whispering the paradox of the salt in food.

The moment we take the wrong path, the landscapes become more and more charming.

Paradoxically we lose our young friends faster.

The paradox that can be explained becomes a rule.

The paradox of hope is the paradox of life-one wants it to come to its end in order to come true.

## DEATH

If we didn't die, we wouldn't be in such a hurry.

People who kill themselves hope there is no After Life.

As if it was not enough that we die, we do it for a long time.

I am dying, as I hate being inactive.

Everybody will leave you alone after you die.

After we die, we will be getting lighter and lighter so as to be able to ascend.

The soldiers that died on the battlefield will continue fighting in heaven.

Among other things I have to do, I have to die.

I will die as well as I can.

We bury our dead as we don't want to hear about metempsychosis anymore.

Death has been taken by surprise since the firing weapons were invented.

We die several times in our life, but we take into consideration only the most successful of them.

Death desecrates life but, it is still regarded as holly.

On the day we don't think about death, we are the closest to it.

I am wondering whether I have died, but there is no one to give me an answer.

Death is a form of neutrality.

I am waiting for my death for different reasons. None of them concerns death directly.

No matter how much we hurry, death still overtakes us.

We accept death the moment we lose our dearest ones.

Death is our permanently postponed meeting with God.

To be young is to enjoy the privilege of thinking about death detachedly.

A double paradox – the symbol of duplicity is the law of a couple.

All I am asking you is to offer something to you.

## PASSION

Passion is the will of permanently fulfilling one's goal.

Only by burning we can show what brightness is.

## SIN

Sin is the silver in which virtues mirror.

When the last census took place, the devils were flabbergasted to find out how few the people were, compared to the number of sins they had in store for them.

Sins are the nails we hammer in the cross of our life delaying our ascension.

For many people happiness is a reason to commit sins.

A sin is pardoned so as the next one to be committed with a clear conscience.

When we sin, we set the devil in us free and he comes back together with some of his brothers.

"God, forgive me for making you responsible for my birth!"

After the Romans offered Christ the crown of thorns, all their laurels became meaningless.

Temptations sent to us by God smell of incense.

Injustice is the first of envies.

Sin is the soul's agony.

## PARENTS AND CHILDREN

A child is love's pleonasm.

At a certain time in their life, even if they make mistakes and are scolded, children dominate their parents. They have the advantage of their young age and the full scope of their future.

Wishing to make their children their friends, parents accuse them of imaginary mistakes so as to subdue them by forgiving them. When children realize this is a hoax, they don't want to be forgiven anymore and the drama begins.

Grandparents love their grandchildren more than they love their children because they have the chance to repeat the same reproaches that were ignored by their offspring when they were the same age.

I appreciate my parents because I know they cannot have another son like me.

Seeing their children parents remember the hot moment when they conceived them. That is why they may avoid telling them how much they love them.

Let's not judge our children as grown-ups, no matter what they will become.

Nine months before I was born, my father loved my mother passionately. I wonder if it were a good idea for me to retire from this world, as I am the product of their love, knowing that my parents often fought afterwards.

Tempting as rebirth may be, I would accept it only if I had the same parents.

Parents are tough with their children because they realize they don't have enough time to explain everything to them at leisure.

To have children is to love correctly.

Almost all children play Mum and Dad, but none of them will ever play divorce.

We owe nothing to our parents, but this nothing is the Buddhist void before our birth.

Children are so much like us that we are ashamed we have made them.

A desired child is born long before its mother gets pregnant.

Gradually the age difference between us and our parents reduces visibly.

Parents are responsible for all their children's actions, irrespective of their age.

If parents loved each other too much, they would not have time to bring up their children.

Parents die before us to show us that nothing is eternal.

The more passionate love we make, the less we want children.

The number of your children equals the number of nights you look at love with different eyes.

Just like Chronos I am throwing up my children, shaped with my teeth.

I dream like a child, and I get sad like a grown-up.

"My love, our child is just me if you had been my mother".

Bedtime stories must be read by parents because they can use their best intonation.

Parents' teachings are the patristics of each family.

**POETRY**

When words are stronger than actions, they turn into poetry.

All our great poets are queuing at Mihai Eminescu's writing table. They carry with them, poems collected while they were travelling the country, poems blown by the wind off the poet's table before he had the chance to sign them.

A great poet realizes that when he/she writes he/she kills his/her feelings.

This is the most beautiful compliment you can pay to a woman: "My lady, allow me to read a line to you. I am in great need of a rhyme".

A poet cannot be confined. This word does not exist in his/her mind.

Elderly poets who die one by one are replaced by some younger ones who have been waiting in a queue for a lifetime enjoying their right of conversing in the booth with the behind-the-bar Muse.

An unsuccessful poet is the poet who writes his/her poems when he/she is too old.

A poet goes to bed in order to dream not because he/she is sleepy.

## POLITICS

Politics is to think about your country from the economic point of view, placing everything in history.
We do politics in order to simplify our living, but we forget that superstructures complicate sequencing impulse.

Any politics asks people to vote. Any fork in a road has a good political capital.

Any philosophy uttered without taking a breath is politics.

Democracy is the progress of freedom.

Like in the Book of Genesis, in politics, in the beginning there was the word.

## FRIENDS

True friends are zero-degree relatives.

If all your friends want to see you on the same day, then you have something to celebrate.

I have a lot of friends, but not all of them know it.

Friendship is the divine substance in us that does not accept the compromise of ignorance.

I betrayed my friends only when I chose them.

One can write a list of friends only by exclusion.

A friend is an envious person who does not understand how I succeeded.

Even man-eaters have friends they cannot swallow.

The true friends do not call you by nicknames.

True friendship - love's practice outside the couple.

I am waiting for my friends as I am waiting for snowfalls. I put on warm clothes and I call you.

A friend hurts you unintentionally, an enemy does you a favour to test you.

Befriend those enemies who are stronger than you are.

Beware of the doctor whose friends are priests!

A friend is that part of you that you let go.

## PROMISES

Any promise can compromise you.

We promise only what we cannot offer.

Life's promises must be observed by us.

A promise is a lie we make at our own risk.

## POWER/STRENGTH

At midday when the Sun is the hottest, actually is the least beautiful.

You are strong when you are aware of all your weak points.

I am so strong that I can see a tunnel traversing any mountain.

To overuse your strength is to weaken it.

Man's greatest strength is his capacity of allowing being defeated.

In the clearness of the sky lies its force of gathering the clouds.

Good things that happen to us are the bad things we succeeded in staying away from.

Everything that pulls you down contributes to your foundation.

A snail, with or without its shell, is equally vulnerable under the cartwheel.

No ship sets sails without a heavy anchor, although it is manufactured for sailing.

Camels know they can cross a desert safely only with the water taken from elsewhere.

## HEAVEN vs HELL

No matter what you are asking God for, don't forget He had offered us the Paradise on His own initiative.

The only way one can progress in heaven is if someone gets out of it.

What is sad about Adam and Eve's story is the fact that even in paradise our sins are not pardoned.

Hell is the heaven with apple trees.

We are supposed to start again our journey to heaven from the beginning, whereas the path to hell is a permanent falling.

Adam and Eve looking for the fruit of knowledge were guided by their thirst for science. This noble intension turned into a sin in the Happiness Realm that blooms only in the body's eyes, and not in the mind's eyes.

Paradise is different for each of us, Hell is the same. Cheers can be amplified, sigh is the foundation.

Some people are so perfect that if they were sent to hell, they would become some decent devils.

We are what God did not want us to be when He banished us from heaven.

Heaven has the grace of receiving us back. God has not started to mould some other humans from clay.

We left Heaven but we have taken the apple tree with us.

The road to heaven is meant to ensure that only the soul will get there.

Most people who want to get to heaven would rather be on good terms with Saint Peter than listen to God.

God did not want us to have heaven in this world so we will not regret when we leave it.

"Honey, God has invited us to go on heaven tour. I suggest packing some apples".

Heaven is angles' pen. Hell is the endless meadow of diabolic temptations.

In the After Life, the lives we saved while on Earth, will be turned into years of heavenly paradise.

The most important verdict God gave in heaven, is not our banishment, but that He didn't allow the Serpent to talk.

Adam and Eve's banishment has taught us, that we can steal from heaven only what we are allowed to.

Adam and Eve showed that the desire to know can only derive from love.

Adam and Eve were banished from Heaven to make all people covet it.

"Honey, the two of us can enter heaven only together. Don't let me wait for you at the gate for years! Don't be late dealing with trivial, routine, ephemeral, cosmetic matters!"

On being banished from Paradise we were punished twice. We were sent into a garden with even more serpents.

God banished us from Heaven. He allowed the serpent to enter it.

We can make a pact with the devil only if he wants to.

Heaven is the orchard with apple trees in blossom. Hell is harvest time.

We give evil a meaning if we analyse it.

## PATIENCE

Life is what does not allow us to be patient.

Women that do not know how to love, do not know how to wait.

We are taught how to be patient, but we are not told what to do with it.

People want us to be erudite, but they do not have patience to listen to what we know.

There are several kinds of patience, but when you are sad, none on them can be applied.

To be patient means to be able to wonder at everything that happens.

I have enough patience not to lose my hope.

Slow and steady wins the race. You need initiative for bigger distances.

If only I had had patience to write when I was talented... but I was in a hurry, afraid that my ideas might have run onto other sheets of paper beautifully wrapped in noble rhymes and no one would have understood their message.

As a reward for my patience, Chronos presented me with a second-handed watch.

Patience is confidence in everything you are waiting for.

Patience waits only for those things it knows will happen to it.

Don't ask time for patience! It will tell you, it is fed up with it.

I am not running toward a goal. People might think I am dodging my responsibilities.

People who are in a hurry postpone their victories.

## MEANNESS

A lot of people think it is a pity not to be mean if they have the opportunity.

When soldiers are given the order to kill their fellow people during a war, they are supposed to fall into a state of trance that separates them from their religious humanness.

We sing in a church in order to clear our voice so as to participate in town riots.

Like the sea that is washing the starfish on the shore, we get rid of evil stuff to look for them in the next wave.

The good belongs to everybody. The evil belongs to each and every one of us.

I am thinking about so many bad things in vain. If any of them had come true, nothing else would be possible.

We are allowed to be mean but only individually.

Some people suffer from value near-sightedness. They can see their fellow people only when the latter fall.

Of all the values people share, only a few evils are worthy of being reproved.

The evil in people externalizes itself, whenever they are not careful.

Meanness is infinitely more sincere than kindness.

## REVENGE

Revenge compromises justice.

Revanchists are the amnesiacs of forgiveness.

## REGRETS

Regrets are the reproaches that forgot their addressees.

Regret is the service entrance of reconciliation.

Regret is the thought that realizes how useless it is.

## RENUNCIATION

The winner that does not intend to go on, is going to wear their laurels in the house.

Nothing in the world can be loved twice. Take care and don't give up on anything you started loving.

Any time you feel like giving up, don't forget that you will have to carry your latest failure with you.

Renunciation protects the species.

Renunciation is not a means of avoiding defeat.

The fact we have been in the same desperate situation since always, does not give me peace of mind.

To feel contented with what you have, means giving up.

If you step aside does not mean you are clearing someone else's way.

## ROMANIA

Romania is such a beautiful country that at every step we have raised flowers as tourist landmarks.

Romania is the teardrop in which the divine smile mirrors itself.

Having children with Dacian women, the Romans acknowledged that they would never have been able to completely conquer Dacia Felix.

## PRAYER

"Lord, although you are in heaven, when I kneel you can hear me better!"

Whenever the evil looked for me, it found me praying.

When I realized how many people died, I realized that to live means praying for them.

God has answered none of my prayers. He thought all of them had been for the After Life.

I am praying that none of my prayers be heard by God. He would find me too weak.

A prayer is the only truth that is stronger if you say it down on your knees.

Prayers have been written for us to know exactly what we can ask God for.

When you make a confession, the priest covers you with his stole to make you feel as if you were alone (or as if he were listening to you from another room).

I am telling the truth as if I were saying a prayer. I know there is someone who is always listening to me.

A prayer has to be said when you are down on your knees, so that the Holy Ghost can come down on us.

On your knees you get ascension.

When one dies one purifies oneself by depositing and when one prays one purifies oneself by evaporating.

We pray down on our knees not to be taller than God.

My soul is paying a short visit to God in heaven to see how He is doing.

"Lord, lead me to the path on which I will be able to walk on my own"

## SACRIFICE

Those who don't understand history are sacrificed.

When what we sacrifice does not surpass the reason of our sacrifice, we don't sacrifice, we lose.

To sacrifice does not mean dying willingly.

Let's behave like flowers. The more heavily they crush us the more scent we release.

If I knew my death made you change at least a bit, I would drink all your poison.

To sacrifice means dying together with your ideas.

Jesus' bride was sufferance; therefore, He did not want to have children.

## HEALTH

Just thinking about health, it weakens.

Health should be encouraged more than convalescence because the latter knows what it has to do.

The doctor's consolation: "You have recovered. You will die from something else."

God tests people through doctors not through illnesses.

To be healthy means fighting with all diseases at the same time.

They would write more treaties about cancer than about Hippocrates.

Health is a means of keeping in touch with the future.

Health is time's mirage running through the carnal desert in order to refresh oneself in the pristine mirror of the oasis of the soul.

You are healthy when each part of your body represents you.

Health is the prostitute that stops visiting us when it notices we have grown old.

Diseases snatch time from our life whereas health offers nothing to us.

According to the World Health Organization health is about physical, mental and social well-being.

There are people who defy pathological condition and become famous because of their handicap.

"Why is it happening to me?" Anyone who is in suffering asks this question. As a physician I want to give you an answer: Each of us suffers from something. We manage to hide it when we are strong, we reveal it when we are weak, but it is permanently with us. This is the noble element of everyone's cross. Isolated from the other people's sufferings we amplify our own. We live mostly in our inner world; therefore, we singularize our anxieties. Illnesses affect both the newly born and the elderly alike. They are the threshold we have to exceed and continue our journey. Let's look around more often!

"This is the beginning of the end." I heard these words in my surgery from a person who was accompanying a patient. He said to me: "Please, doctor examine him. I think he has the beginning of the end" I think this is the definition of an illness: the start of decline, the first sign of erosion.

That part of illness that surrenders, is called healing.

## KISS

Love has changed the status of lips.

"How much happiness people find in a kiss!" God exclaims as he knows he banished us from Heaven because of our thirst for knowledge.

When we kiss it is important what we do with our hands.

The problem with love is about what we do with our time between kisses.

In love, a kiss is not a good beginning.

Any kiss is memory's moment of oblivion.

For a lot of people "I love you" means asking for permission to kiss.

A kiss can be declined, love cannot.

When the riot is given a kiss of love, they turn it into passion.

A kiss is a sacrifice on the altar of the lips.

A kiss is our mistake of loving by showing.

A kiss is the air we blow into love's balloon.

A kiss is love's breathing.

## WRITING

I have been writing to prove I am a very resourceful man.

Whenever I talk without writing I am like the library in Alexandria without flames.

I am going to bury my writings as I want to hear you shout sometime later, "I have found the continuation of the Bible".

The strength to write has been given to me by the incomplete works I am reading.

When you write you take time's place. You run for eternity. You accept the uselessness of your discourse with the people around you, with your present time.
You are building a new history for you. You place yourself in the future without being dead.

I am writing so passionately that I am tearing the sheets of paper under my pen.
Come and read them quickly while I am writing!

If I had known how to write without inspiration, I would have written well from the very beginning.

When you realize how much you can create in solitude you come to love it.

Solitude is the price one has to pay to be admired.

I am the philosopher at the end of an idea.

As I am writing, the pile of manuscripts is getting heavier and heavier, so I am no longer able to lift it. My body has grown old. It is full of knowledge.

I would stop signing my writings if I were not afraid of being like too many other classic writers.

My plays are so difficult, that when the season opens, they will hand down some brochures with the text to help people understand them, a practice similar to librettos sung in a foreign language.

I would like to write a romance, but one of my girlfriends has stolen all my sheets of paper.

Since I started writing, people have stopped telling me my writings are poor. They have been telling me they do not understand me.

People who write because they can't help it, are suicidal, not writers. A real writer has a thousand possible options and he/she chooses to write. When he/she has only one option left he/she prefers either to commit suicide, like Esenin for instance, who had written poems with his own blood for a day, or to die in the end.

I write because written paper burns better.

I like what I write. I risk becoming my own reader.

I am an Einstein of the spirit. Only the truths I refuse to find out, are alien to me.

A writer is like an ink fish. His/her life is dipped in ink.

I am not saying new things. I am saying things that have not been heard before.

"Can you do anything else apart from writing poems?" someone asked me once.
"Of course, I can. I can read them to you" I answered.

I am playing with the vowels since I constantly force them not to leave the page.

The fame of writing does not have to exceed the success of being read.

I constantly forget my name; therefore, I have to write it down on my books.

I don't like being seen when I am writing. It is as if I were naked.

When I write poems, I resemble those parents who buy clothes for their children as if they were for them.

I waste my time writing, but I don't mind. The alternative would have been to fight with people.

I am the writer, and you are my readers. One of us has made the wrong choice.

Writing is the vulnerable side of thought.

## FELLOW PEOPLE

By respecting a human being, you acknowledge her/his divine affiliation.

We depend on other people inasmuch they don't understand it.

The most powerful pressures that influence us are the atmospheric ones and the most sensitive are the human ones.

Some people like doing what depends on us.

Every day we lose a bit of our ego. We get something from the collective ego. The benefit is reciprocal.

People who move house and do not tell us about it, have done it on purpose.

The important people are those whose absence is notice before you are calling the roll.

Everything we reproach with our fellow people used to intrigue us.

We are self-confident because we have been disappointed by the others for a long time.

It is worth loving all the people if at least one of them loves you.

Personal charm is, in fact, collective. You are liked by someone who has understood you and this happens only if you reveal yourself.

The fact I don't know most inhabitants of this Small Planet certifies the uselessness of my existence.

I used to be confined in the world and I have escaped due to you.

## FEELINGS

Let's not philosophize on our feelings, it is enough we have them.

Any state of mind not fully lived can be taken for melancholy.

If you ask me to love you, don't ask me why.

My heart is the woman who refused to marry me.

Feelings are our soul's early fruit.

A feeling is the hypocrisy of a thought.

Thoughts that die become feelings.

Traditions are feelings that externalize themselves not to be forgotten.

Keep your own insults for you! Your feelings are enough for me.

To be upset with people is like hurting God.

We are sentimental only if we are realistic enough to take feelings seriously.

Stewed love reminds me of potato stew. Feelings must be explosive.

Feelings are soul's metaphors.

Our feelings have a fixed idea, ourselves.

We are not responsible for our feelings, only for their externalization.

The feelings we share are the steadiest.

Feelings must be sustained with ideas.

I have educated my feelings to obey me. Those that refuse to do it are allowed to fall in love.

Feelings' approval needs pain's seal and signature.

If we didn't have hands, our love would rely mostly on feelings.

Gestures are the feelings that cannot desert us.

Sentimentalism is soul's bodybuilding.

To love means knowing your feelings by heart.

## SEXUALITY

If in the verse: "Love and fill the earth!" God had thought about physical love, He would have added:" While you are still young".

"My sweetheart, I love you so much that I am caressing the colours of your clothes. I love caressing your red most often"

Love is a mirage that may get pregnant.

Mistresses are the twigs that sustain love's fire. The first flame can only make them burn brighter but when it has devoured the last one, it will die out scattering its ashes.

When we make love our clothes, spread all around the bed, seem to belong to some children who suddenly felt so sleepy that they didn't have time to undress at leisure and fold their clothes carefully.

Love is like hunger. It must be satisfied several times a day.

Like a snake hidden in the bosom I am biting into the flesh I love.

People who do not have the courage to say they love each other, are in love, and thus they make love from the very beginning.

In love, "far" means a distance larger than a bed.

Nature does not let us postpone our love.

At night love declarations seem more sincere.

A dress both excites and postpones love at the same time.

If you want to keep love, you have to participate in it with all your body.

King Danaos' mistake was that he asked the Danaids to kill their husbands at night when they were making love.

Bed is lovers' pedestal.

Our antagonistic sides meet when we make love.

A vast number of loves would die if we multiplied through spores.

What a pity we love each other only to make love!

There are so many women in my love that I asked them to stop being stout.

Make me love you and I will gladly love you, being convinced you really wanted me.

A mistress will claim rewards even for things she did not do.

To give up on love is like presuming you were born by division.

Love that cannot wait is instinct.

Loving each other passionately, we give birth to warlike children.

There are a lot of loves precipitated by rain.

Love is the metaphysics of a kiss.

Love is an aphrodisiac of conscience.

Peeps are Cupid's glimpses, out of which he made his arrows.

I have heard that if we make love standing, we get taller. We didn't know it and we have changed about three beds so far.

A dumb man who rapes a woman should not be punished. He simply wants to show his love for her.

A man who cannot convince a woman to take off her clothes, should go to war.

## SAINTS

Holy relics outside a tomb are more worshiped than kings' golden crypts.

God does not know about Hell because no angel had the courage to tell Him about it.

Saints are the humble gods of Christianity.

Job believed that we would leave this world exactly as we came into it. This is in fact his drama. We must leave it the people must be better.

By the time you get to God, saints will have judged you, so that our Maker does not take you over right away.

A dragon may be in an icon, but only when Saint George defeats it.

"It is no use being alone when you die" said the icon painter and started working busily.

## SINCERITY

If we told only the truth, we would speak much less.

The simultaneity of actions compromises their spontaneity.

Allow me to tell you the truth about me and you will find out untrue things, too.

I admit my guilt, but I don't know in front of whom.

Let's be openhearted. Flowers are beautiful because they are open.

## SOLITUDE

Solitude is the confrontation with all our ideas.

We would not pluck the flower if it were the only one in the garden.

We are all trying to build a world where we could belong.

I hate solitude but I desire to see you leave.

I am sure of myself, I am not sure of you.

I say I am alone, but in fact I am not saying it to myself.

Solitude is a trap. You can get out of it, but you are always injured.

The enemy of solitude is waging a Holy War.

I need no one around me, but if you want me to tell it to you, you have to come after me.

The real solitude is when your mother asks you whether you want a sibling.

I am so lonely that even solitude ignores me.

I don't succeed in being alone. Enemies never forget me.

To be alone is to share your solitude with God.

In solitude we can be more useful to ourselves.

We share solitude as we share a loaf of bread. Each of us takes more than he/ she deserves.

The solitude I wanted came accompanied.

Solitude is to get drunk with oneself.

From the Realm of Solitude, I came back with a friend - I have found myself.

When solitude starts knowing us, it gets sad.

We are not alone if our solitude is understood by the others.

Even those who love solitude cry for help.

Any love amplifies your solitude at a certain moment.

Any solitude can give birth to a religion when it becomes tempting for the others as well.

My solitude can hold the whole world.

"My sweetheart, my presence in you is so discrete, that I can hear you complaining of solitude."

A lonely man always waits for someone.

I want to be alone, and you gather around me asking me why.

Solitude is a condition when soul makes friends.

Wherever I go, solitude calls me back.

Those who cannot find a remedy in solitude are not pleased with themselves.

Other people's solitude bores me more than my own.

We would not be alone without love, but we would feel solitude more acutely.

In solitude a watch measures sadness, not time.

You are alone when your enemies forget you.

I am the only one who can understand my despairs.

## SUICIDE

If someone commits suicide, they are stronger than life, but they become the prisoners of death.

Suicidal people die avidly.

Suicidal people may include a lot of our friends, but none of them is a true friend.

If you try to convince a suicidal man/woman to give up on their intension, you may offer them an extra reason for doing it.

People who want to die, have lived in vain.

Committing suicide is our most adamant answer to life.

When you are at a loss and don't know what to do, it is advisable that you should not commit suicide. You may change your mind later.

## SLEEP

We seem so ignorant when we sleep, but thus we charge ourselves with a lot of energy.

If we could see how much time we spend sleeping, we would get bored of ourselves.

## HOPE

Hope is the fair-play of failure.

To hope is to respect your future.

Hope is that part of us that does not accept its destiny.

Hope is our pride facing the future.

Projects are our hopes written down on paper.

Set your heart on something, but don't leave it there.

I have found my equilibrium. I started being indifferent to my hopes.

I am Achilles running after the turtle. I cannot catch up with my hopes.

Any hope is the beginning of disillusionment.

Hope is soul's capital of ambition.

The Little Prince inside us hopes that on our Soul's Planet flowers will be able to develop their roots before their seeds.

Hopes trouble my sorrows.

The hope while you are patient will dissipate while you are waiting.

Everything I lost while hoping I have found again in ambition.

Hopes are the coloured balloons we are holding. When they rise, we are lost.

If you want to kill a hope, all you have to do, is to give it a try.

Sometimes hopes that are not up to you, come true quicker.

Hope is the present we are not sure whether to receive or not.

Hope is the dream you believe in, despair is the dream you used to believe in.

Hope is the hand that life reaches out for us.

Melancholic people set their heart on the past.

My death is so far away that I cannot even catch a glimpse of it among so many hopes.

Our hopes come true chronologically with our belief in them.

Hopes feed on illusions.

A hope inspirationally placed in time has all the chances of coming true.

If you don't want to waste a hope, you have to keep it alive among some others.

If you hope, you will not have everything, but you will think about everything.

A hope that does not disappoint us is a plan well-conceived.

Only those people whom we can tell lies to, can be made to hope.

I pity those whose hopes do not concern them.

To get something means killing another hope.

A hopeless beginning is the continuation of a disappointment.

To value only those hopes that come true, means finding joy only in those flowers that you can pluck.

## SUFFERING

Suffering is the theophany of pain.

Suffering is the squeaks of the Pearly Gates.

Something must have died inside me, otherwise I cannot explain why my body is so heavy.

Pain is the ecstasy of sufferance.

Any pain that has gone, seems impossible for you to bear again.

Pain is the force we still have when we have lost confidence.

The pains that still hurt have not been self-inflicted.

Pain keeps you awake.

Pains like being kept alive. They don't come by themselves.

The road to sufferance takes you beyond it.

Other people's sufferings teach me patience. Mine teaches me hope.

Love and suffering are both measured in tears.

Despair consists only of previous happy moments.

Suffering is like life. As long as we have it, we live it.

Suffering is a way of measuring patience.

Suffering is the age that is not measured in years.

No matter how terrifying a storm may be the wave that is in a hurry cannot overtake the one in front of it.

## SOUL

Soul is the tear God has dripped in each of us.

"God, forgive me, I have smeared my soul with my body."

The soul has to fold its wings in order to live in a body.

The soul is the beauty one cannot see.

The soul is the woman on whom God has put some expensive clothes.

Soul stones, like the kidney stones have to be removed.

Repentance weakens the soul. Contrition smears it with blood. Self-forgiveness heals it.

The purest soul is the soul that does not belong to the body.

I enjoy myself in my soul like in a small pub. When I get drunk, I wake up.

The stronger I am, the more fearful of me my soul is.

Soul is the time that has got used to suffering from hunger.

"Lord, please come into my small, my ugly and unwelcoming soul! Don't forget, you have made it like that."

Our soul gets sad any time we promise it a transient happiness.

A murderer first kills his/ her soul.

Any time we put on clothes our soul sweats.

When the tribes of my soul are cheering a master that is to put the flesh of my body in spears, I tell them they are going to have a master like that only after I have died.

The soul's witness is the body. It doesn't have the guts to testify.

## SILENCE

Just think how many outstanding forefathers have fallen silent, for us to be able to speak.

I am talking, so I can hide the silences.

I am talking so as to dissipate the suspicions that I am dumb.

The distance between people is measured in their silences.

I have nothing against, the least I can do is to refrain myself.

I won't say anything, for fear I might compromise my silence.

Silence is a guilty witness.

Silence, I will never desecrate you with words.

To learn how to keep silent means getting used to dying.

Silence is the fastest rumour.

Silence is a such soft yell to be heard.

## THEORY

The best treaties are not enough to learn how to swim.

Theory is the philosophy of reality.

Problems that lose their bodies turn into ideas.

## TIME

Time is an enemy that understands me.

We are wasting our time by living.

Wasted time doubles our life.

I arrived in time lest my delay might not be noticed.

If we are given breathing time, we can arrive in time.

To come holding a watch in your hand doesn't mean you're coming in time.

Spring is very impressed by our way of waiting for it, and thus, it never comes in time.

Pressed by time we become shadows.

I am pouring water into my sandglass to make the sand denser.

We start living the moment we start fighting with time.

We could steal time only from sleep and death, but this can be easily noticed.

Every time we have a little free time we die.

Time invented the people the moment it wanted to devour stones and lost its teeth. Its fear persisted. That is why, it first caresses us, and then it swallows us very carefully.

Desperate people come back to their pre-existence period, raising stone monuments to defy time. Chronos knows them well and glorifies them for years, but he is still pleased to feed just on heroes.

I hate people who are in a hurry, as they want to skip stages. But life is deep water. It does not have stepping-stones for you to cross it. To those who are in a hurry I recommend to swim as fast as they can and be aware of the fact that water in its entirety will wet them, and I, that am just contemplating, I will also benefit from it.

While brainwaves are coming to me, I am reading, as I hate wasting time.

As long as we consider time a benchmark, it will elapse implacably.

If time didn't exist, sandglasses would have been invented only for sifting sand.

At the end of time a man can only beg for a couple of seconds.

Time is the watch with a gaining rate.

Time proves its supremacy by passing.

The fact that a sandglass can be turned upside down, pleads for immortality.

Everything happens at the right time, but unfortunately nothing happens at our time.

Time is the only wonder that lasts longer than three days.

We think highly of time; therefore, we use watches as jewels.

If time didn't pass so quickly, we would get old in a year.

"Better late than never" is the syntagm that makes death feel useful.

Only if you lose your watch on your way can you arrive before time.

Time stops when man moves faster.

The better friend time is to us, the more it ignores us.

We cannot face time just by looking at the watch.

We celebrate our birthdays, although Chronos rubs his hands.

We live long despite wasting time.

In our fight with time, just like a watch, we have been wound back to the beginning

"My son, you should never have anything to do with me" Time told me presenting a watch to me.

We win times not time.

Time is patient only with those who hurry it up.

Time holds world speed record, no matter how much we delay its start.

Everything that happens to us, observes only time's laws.

We are the moments of a changing time.

We are in such a hurry, as if we lived our entire life standing.

A watch is time's pulse.

To be born prematurely means asking the doctors, whether it makes any sense to stay alive.

Regret is desire eaten by time.

Eternity is the moment that has not arrived yet.

A watch is Chronos' mark on any mortal's arm.

Moment is time's transience.

Things happen so fast, that we hardly have time to tell them.

People who do not know how to spend their spare time, say they are busy.

Life is time thrown at us by gods

Chronology is time's genealogy.

An ancient man sacrificed a ring in order to thank Fate for his Happiness, whereas we sacrifice our lifetime.

Haste is running counter clockwise.

## YOUTH

When you are young you exclude death from your plans.

We are not young unless our youth is romantic.

We are young as long as our children are still playing with us.

But for wisdom, I would have liked to stay young my whole life.

To be young is to say that all your vanities are loves.

Youth, that doesn't set itself to do some impossible things, has matured too soon.

No other number seems bigger to me than the one that represents our age.

As long as physical love gives us peace, we are still young.

Our chance is not to stay young, but to wish for it.

Youth is the soul that God anointed our body with.

You are not young as long as you do not benefit from all youth's trumps.

Youth turns us into love's offering.

You are still young if your biological life expectancy is a lifetime.

It is nice to tell somebody that he/she is young, but not when you appreciate his/her work.

## BETRAYAL

Murderers boast about being traitors, and they don't lie.

A traitor benefits from the victory of neither party.

Traitors shouldn't be looked for too far away.

## PAST

Past seems short to us because we eliminate hopes from it.

By going back into the past, we forget about the present, then that past comes back.

Asking people to forget their past, is like asking them to forget who they are.

To feel sorry is like turning the hands of time in vain.

You can get over your past only by looking into your future, by remembering what it is going to happen. Be careful, though. When the wings of future start flapping, it already becomes past.

If tomorrow looks alike yesterday, then yesterday is not over yet.

If you go back into the past and this does not show on you, then you have a steady character.

Past is the future one has already lived.

Past is future's gravitational force.

Present is everything left for us from the past.

A reproach is a slap that sends you back into the past.

## SORROW

The sorrow you don't ignore gives you sad explanations.

The real sorrow doesn't rely on tears.

It is sad that life asks us so much evidence of our love for it.

We find jokes funnier when we are sad.

Sorrow is so bitter that even if it is sweetened with books, it becomes erudition not happiness.

Let's never be the cause of our own sorrow.

God is so sad when He sees that human, the paragon of His creation, is so helpless.

It is nice to be sad, but you are not the only one.

My guardian angel told me he would leave me in a devil's care for a while. My melancholy saddens him.

It is sadder not to be right than not to be believed.

Let's not be alone! Sorrow should be enjoyed in groups.

I am so sad I could dance to Mozart's Requiem like Zorba to sirtakis.

Sorrow is the reward of you having smiled.

Sorrow is the accountancy of pains.

The mechanism of sorrow cannot be triggered off automatically.

Our birth has a lugubrious verso.

Transposition is the capacity of sharing joy and escaping from your own sorrow.

We live our life as if it were someone else's and thus, we experience the regret of memories.

Eyes hold body's entire sorrow.

When we don't fight against our own sorrow, we cause it ourselves.

Lamentation is pestering sorrow.

Unhappiness is a form of the future that we don't want.

Disappointment is the exile of hopes.

Frustration is the economy of despair.

A grumpy man is happy at the thought that he will die.

## ARROGANCE

The generals' mistake is their belief that mothers give birth to soldiers.

Ambition converted into pride refuses to give up on its title.

Arrogance is a bridge you build in order to tread on people, instead of walking among them.

The unfulfilled ambitions turn into vanities.

If the lioness had believed, just for a moment, that her husband is the King of animals, she would have chosen a more interesting fur.

We talk to the gods every time we have a fight with God.

## BODY

God refused to offer human any physical capability because the latter would have felt tempted to develop this feature and would have stopped thinking.

Lungs don't know that actually we do not breathe for them.

We cannot see blood, our vital liquid. We are not allowed to deepen our knowledge on what keeps us alive.

## OBLIVION

Time is an enemy only to those who forget.

Everything we forget can make us younger.

Oblivion is the eyesight of amnesia.

Everything that does not last long, is forgotten.

Some people are so vainglorious that they say they have forgotten what they don't know.

Our stiffness when we die has nothing of the impetuous labour with which we came into this world.

The most powerful man forgets the soonest.

I want to write down two lists: one of the things I am not allowed to forget and the other one of what I frequently omit. If the two lists overlap, I am going to give up on the former.

"You are sentenced to oblivion." Let's admit that this is not the heaviest sentence.

A lot of people forget that life includes childhood as well.

If people forget your name, to change it is not the best solution.

## HATRED

If you hate me, it is enough for me. Forgive me!

I love all the women who hate me. They hate me because I used to love them.

The people I detest are the people I used to love by mistake. I can be sincere with them, only if I betray them, if I let them down.

Even if you hate me, you don't teach me what hatred is!

Do what you want with me, but don't hate me!

I miss you when I hate myself.

We are too much dependent on love to hate all life long.

## ETERNITY

Eternity is time's insanity of competing against itself.

When I die, I would like to hear people say: "A great future is in store for you."

It is my parents' merit of having brought me into this world, it is God's merit of keeping me alive and it is my merit if I succeed in staying in people's hearts.

The After Life was set up because we will give up on everything that is physical. The infinite is the volatilization of the matter.

I live. God is waiting for me in the sky to confirm it.

"Lord, I am so afraid that my current life is the after-life."

I am grateful to the moment that it passes by. It shows me the way to eternity.

Eternity is not extraordinary. It needs time, as we do, in order to exist.

Compared to eternity, life is the only moment that is worth living.

If you live only till the last moment of your life, you can say you were not even born.

Even in the After Life it is advisable to be sceptical since no one else died for you.

At a certain age we can say we still have a death waiting for us to make us happy.

I don't know where God will post me from this world.

As long as I belong to this world, I cannot understand it. I keep cramming ideas dedicated to my beginning of eternity preparing the accession of my judgmental soul. The wheat ear cannot claim the sheaf of wheat, but it lays all its hope in the harmony of bread.

Enjoy the sap of the fruits I am offering to you to the full! I am offering them to you, so the wood stays dry the moment my old trunk will plunge into the water of eternity. It is its only chance to float.

## LIFE

Life is death that makes a little time for it.

Life is the pilgrimage to your own tomb.

Life is a trap for ideals

Life is a perfect murder.

Life is a joke that death seizes in a chance.

Life doesn't offer solutions, it offers situations.

Hope is our pride facing the future.

Life is a guideline to the possible ways of dying.

We participate as victims in our life.

Life is the haste to live.

If we are fed up with life, it doesn't mean we have to die.

We keep living in spite of our more and more negative opinions on life.

Life is the practical joke the destiny plays on us.

The time that time makes for us is called life.

Life is like this: it is advisable that you should not need you, and nevertheless you should be useful to yourself.

We witness all opportunities in our life.

Life is not willing to make any biological concession to us.

I know I am innocent, but I accept to live.

People took me seriously when I told them that I lived, but when I told them I wouldn't live long they ignored me.

I was destined to be born in a period when I managed to fake death and consequently everything I lived afterwards seemed of little account.

I love being active. Death sees me, leaves me alone and says, "Move on!"

I am living my life to the full. It is my way of writing my memoires for those who don't have time to read them.

My life is a happy obituary and my enemies precipitate to conclude it with 'Many Happy Returns!"

My life started well. I was born healthy.

Who keeps on lying to each other that we are alive? At night when all of you are sleeping, I can see the sky is full of vigil stars.

With every sunrise, God asks us to live one more day.

What are we living for when some others will start our life from the beginning?

I go through life like a fish that swims without tasting water.

Life is eternity's line of action.

Life is the fight with time.

Life is eternity but for a long time we do not regard it as transient.

If life is asking you for details, it means it got bored with you.

All we want from life are those things it has never given us before.

Life jokes with people who would tell it "You are young."

Life is guilty and knowing it quite well, it accepts any insult.

Life's traffic lights are painted green, but they all show red any way you want to go.

No one gets a prize in life. Losers are punished, though.

All we want from life is to keep its word.

Life gives us the leftovers of the others.

My amendment to life is the following: Stop being so wicked for I did not ask to be born!

When we ask something from life it behaves like a neighbour. It reminds us that we owe to it.

As people know they are given this life, they are looking for new tiebreakers.

We build our life with our own hands; therefore, our handprints stay on our face as wrinkles.

We are the witnesses of our own life and the judges of the other people's life.

Life is in love with us, but it thinks about death.

The essence of life is to live it as if you had imagined it before you were not born yet.

Life is not the most extraordinary thing that can happen to us.

We owe life a death. I pity those who intend to pay for it in time.

If we don't try to change Life, it will become a hell for us to know what to expect when it is over.

I don't think that nine months is enough for us to get prepared in order to come into this world.

I owe to life so much that I feel ashamed to tell it that I am going to die.

All the things that really happen to us are conjugations of the verb "to be". The other verbs do not have any semantic value for the soul.

Life is a whore and no matter how many times you kiss her, she will not open her legs.

My life didn't have me in mind.

Life is like Pythagoras' theorem. It has been like that since the beginning of the world. it is easy to understand it, you have understood it, but you have never applied it.

We live for real only those parts of our life's events that we understand.

Life is a race. It does not matter how many contestants you take over, but how many laps you have run.

Life is the journey in which we would like to get lost only to make it last longer.

We are the makers of our own life.

Our life has pink and blue periods just like Picasso's paintings.

To talk about your life is as dangerous as to live it.

Life is like water you are holding in your cupped hands. No matter how tight you close them you still lose it.

Life is a book. The more cultured you are the longer it takes you to read it.

Life is a book you succeed in reading only if you take your time.

We value life in its raw form, as the opposite to death.

Life is the bullfighting in which the bulls have golden horns, but it is still a bullfighting.

The path of our life is a zigzag. The unlived events are hatched by death.

We can ask life for anything, but for nothing eternal.

Life has been my first unpleasant experience.

Life monotony despairs us but we have accepted, without demur, not to be allowed to create a new menu every day.

Every day I pay a tribute because I insist on living.

'I have had enough of this life" – says the Buddhist during his fifth reincarnation.

I quarrel with life every day and the next day I give it right.

Life is a beautiful woman, who little by little and day by day, is prostituting. In the end she loses her beauty, but she becomes a perfect prostitute.

The longer you live, the more reasons to die for, you will find.

We build our life using the logs of death, and then we have the impudence to ask why it did not last.

Life is an assorted pizza. Someone sitting at a table next to us is eating spaghetti.

You can ask from life only what you owed to it.

As life is an in-sight display check, any mistake can be seen. "We give you the interest on the spot" the bank officers worn me as soon as they notice my mistake. I avoid carrying a large sum of money with me, but it is not advisable to salt my account either, as I myself will answer to it. A so-called wise guy waiting in the queue suddenly says, "Sir, if you are so undecided, exchange everything into hard currency!"

We are the comedians of our own life, waiting for tragedy fans to applaud us.

If we take advantage of our life, it means we have not understood it.

The drama of our life is that we are building a world in which our children will live.

I enter my life the same as a moment enters a watch, pushed by the next one.

Starting with a certain moment our life can go on without us.

It is more and more difficult for life to stand us.

God gives us an honest choice namely life. We start weaving a lot of plots around it.

Life with its great disappointments is a temptation. We are guilty only when we leave this world.

Life should not be lived only for the sake of living it till its end.

Life has the end that suits it.

Life sometimes has impossible expectations from us.

If we were asked to write down our entire life story, we would write down only our birthplace, the names of our parents and the names of our children.

We witness some important events in our life.

Life takes counsel with us only in essential problems.

Let's not reproach today for anything, let's reproach only for the life we have lived so far.

Let's not allow our life to miss us, for any departure is a pretext for possible betrayal.

Life told me: "Leave me alone if you want to live well with me."

It is important how our life influences the people around us.

# VICTORY

We have to repeat our victories in order to convince ourselves they are real.

Victories are grown-ups' toys.

The way to victory is touch-and-go.

The desire to win should have nothing to do with fear of failure.

Success is the postponement of victory.

Our genuine achievements in life are already made by others and we fall in love with them.

The areas where you have been unsuccessful should be tried. They may have become more flexible in the meantime.

Success is a sweet singing bird and if it also flies, then it is glory.

Success is an induced feat.

Victory oughtn't to be dedicated to anybody, otherwise failure would have been his /her responsibility, too.

Failure is the trampoline of success.

No achievement is one hundred per cent ours.

Presumably, a failure may turn into a victory the same as a success may repeat itself.

If we have not been defeated, it is the opponent's merit as well.

We deserve a failure that we did not anticipate.

To be defeated by a weaker opponent does good to your pride and harms your morale.

Repeated victories could be considered a single victory that may become eternal.

Our complexes derive mostly from the other people's failures.

Failures separate us from dreams.

The loser boasts he/ she has tried harder than the winner.

The losers are on the podium in the winners' hearts.

Whoever controverts their victory deserves it.

Any ransom promised before the victory humiliates.

Victory is the limit of fight.

To win means giving up fighting since you are going to be rewarded.

# FUTURE

Future is time's optimism.

A melancholic person asks future to repair their past.

We are waiting for the future as if it had promised something to us.

Fate doesn't hesitate to give you all the things you haven't asked from it.

Past is the noblest form of choosing our future.

Any child that grows up, does it in order step in our shoes.

Future is the past waiting for us.

Tomorrow belongs to those who treasure today.

Future is the form of present we opt for.

All my projects have been fulfilled. Now it is ambitions' turn.

The future that starts today is more reliable than the future that starts tomorrow.

Our tragedy is that we are the future of a world that has not come to an end.

The future is too far from us to see us. We must wave at it.

Don't ask from future just everything it has promised to you!

Future is the only way one can ignore the past.

We can lie to the future as long as it hasn't come.

We are the most distant part of our future.

The future that does not need the past is uncertain.

"What would you do if the world finished tomorrow?"
"I'll tell you the day after tomorrow."

## VICES

Girls do not inherit their mother's lovers, but the number of them.

My only form of disdain is the ardour with which I am facing evil things.

People who cannot cure their vices, glory in them.

Vices care about their victims more than love does.

Passions were vices if sufferings were their consequences and not a primordial for them.

Some people have perfected their vices to such an extent that if you want to make them aware of them, you have to take them from their happy and prosperous world into the world of humiliations and shortages and in this medium, they will prove themselves useless.

No thief has stolen enough to forget his/her vice.

Thieves envy liars because the latter have more time in their hands.

I am not thirsty enough to drink water.

## GUILT

Guilt is an act of injustice to your own person, that started in the past.

It is easy for us to choose some people to represent us, when it comes about a common guilt.

The life we overlook calls to thank us.

We admit our guilt only through the perspective of its consequences.

We feel so guilty towards ourselves, that we are afraid to do something and get involved in.

If you feel guilty you are going to die, you will end by committing suicide.

Apologies make guilt seem more agreeable, but they also intensify it.

If we were not guilty, apologies would turn into gratifications.

The husband who comes home with his stomach full, blames the food that has got cold while he was being waited for.

We are forgiven if we fail in our extraordinary plans, but we are not excused if we don't have extraordinary plans.

When things go bad it is easy to find scapegoats.

The guilt belongs only to the person who does not admit it.

One guilt any less and the earth would be spinning faster.

Guilt is a homage, something we consider we could have done better.

When they ask the question "Whose guilt is bigger than mine?" you should answer.

Of the original sin, our share of guilt stands out itself bearing the shape of our body that corrupts us every moment.

If we cannot pinpoint whose guilt it is, then it belongs to us.

The cannibals' excuse is that they eat without salt.

Most of us want to be pardoned before they are judged.

Those who forget their promises cannot be condemned for not keeping them.

Regret always has time on its side.

Those who are responsible for our birth should also bring us up.

The best accomplices are those who don't know quite well what they are involved in.

The shared guilt does not diminish, it multiplies.

Who feels responsible is the first to take the floor.

Even a collective guilt has to be punished individually.

To be guilty means being the talk of the town.

Each guilty part has a very acute sense of comparison.

We are all culpable of that part of our destiny lying ahead of us and not met yet.

The fact that punishments are standardized, do not prevent the culprits from being inventive.

The courage of asking for an apology is not given by the guilt.

The guilt is the permanent state of equilibrium between good and evil.

## DREAM

If you chase wild geese, you may be accidently shot.

The wishes that do not come true, allow us to approach other dreams which we were not aware of before.

I participate in my dreams only by switching the light off.

To dream means having the future on your side.

To dream means having an ideal.

The most beautiful dream is that one that doesn't choose its setting.

We have such a modest dream that we do not hesitate to welcome it wearing inelegant pyjamas.

When you dream yourself, it means you have entered someone else's dream.

A dream that started from sorrow has a long life.

It is a shame to lie down to sleep not to dream.

A dream can kill the outside reality, handling it with kid gloves.

The dreamer's body is the featherless wing searching for the air currents in order to rise.

Dream if you want to avoid insomnias!

Sleep is the shadow against which dreams project themselves.

If we fell asleep in the church, we would dream ourselves dead.

We dream in order to give our phantasms a meaning.

We are most useful to dreams when we are sleeping. We have to wait for the sublime ones.

Sleep never asks me what dream I would choose.

To dream means making use of my entire inner world, giving no chance to the outside world.

I can't make my dreams come true if no one takes them seriously.

Sleep is the only real support of dream.

I am dreaming when the others think I am sleeping.

We sleep only in those nights when someone tells us "Good night!".

If some of our dreams come true, it means we don't sleep in vain.

Sleep is the chromatics of dream.

Sleep is a happy shipwreck.

If our dreams contained more truth, lies would stop making fun of them.

I sleep with the woman I am dreaming.

If only one of my dreams came true, then, consequently, all of them would.

Without dreams night would seem darker to us.

Our calculations destroy our ideals.

The dreams we don't believe in are borrowed.

Not only is a dream abstract, but people are looking for new significances.

## WILL

To know what you want is more important than to know what to do.

The fact that we want to win does not say too much about our will.

Our personality depends on the will's mortar used to cover our weaknesses.

Will is thought's mania.

Your will is strong if you go into the desert although you are already thirsty.

Will is to believe in oneself more than the others do.

## SMILE

We smile although it requires the effort of the muscles.

A smile is a woman's main means of refusal.

## FLIGHT

I won't show you how I fly unless you lower your rifles aiming at the sky.

No bird sings while flying.

Catch a bird, stick its feathers the other way round and when you scare it, it will fly to you.

A bird rises if it takes off and strikes the air.

If you try too hard to fly, you will meet no angels during your flight.

No bird can get cold feet after it started flying.

I wish I had wings, not to fly with, but to understand what birds feel like when they are not able to fly any more.

Birds' claws hinder their flight.

No matter how big a bird may build its nest, it will never be able to fly in it.

Only after man invented the plane, did he realize he would never be able to be a bird.

Birds are the sky's fissures.

Fog is the marks left in the air by the snails that tried to fly during the rain.

## MISCELLANEA

Eagles are the chance the cliffs had not to be alone.

But for the mermaids, the cloth industry would not have prospered.

If you sow foreign fields, you will share your meals.

Effect is what is left from a cause.

A rule that cannot be extended is a postulate.

Depth is the ideal of precipice.

Morality is the defence that ascends us.

Desert is the land ploughed by the sun.

Infinite is the cloudless sky.

The shadow is the train of a dress on which the devils tread.

A happy-ending story is that one that ends as it started.

A slap on one's cheek is a caress performed in a hurry.

The widely circulated languages are the advice of the few earthlings who didn't have room in the Babel Tower.

The foundation is the earth desire to know we are going to have a house built.

Any stereotype bores us if we are not careful to use it in the right context.

Everything that happens to us has no footnotes for explanations.

If we talked only about our achievements, we would start working sooner.

europe books

CPSIA information can be obtained
at www.ICGtesting.com
Printed in the USA
LVHW101139191122
733278LV00024B/1374

9 791220 120005